D0368804

Labor Revolt in Alabama

Robert David Ward
William Warren Rogers

Labor Revolt in Alabama:

The Great Strike of 1894

SOUTHERN HISTORICAL PUBLICATION #9
UNIVERSITY OF ALABAMA PRESS
University, Alabama

This book is for Lillian Kiber Ward
and Harry E. and Mittie Pate Rogers

Contents

Preface

Few subjects in Southern history have been less explored than the labor movement between 1865 and 1900. This book focuses on the Alabama coal miner strike (and to a lesser degree on the strike by railroad workers) of 1894. Because of its mineral deposits in the Birmingham area, Alabama became industrialized before the turn of the century. The strike of 1894 was complex in that it pitted a union movement with its urban and industrial ideas against an agrarian society largely rural and unacquainted with the aspirations of labor. Attempts at unionization came at a highly unfortunate time; the economic depression that hit the nation in 1893 was felt with full force in 1894. The distress in the South was particularly acute. Alabama was still recovering from the difficulties of Reconstruction when the panic struck.

In addition to the one clear-cut conflict between management and labor, the issue of wages, the Alabama strike involved the employment of Negroes as strikebreakers, the question of convict labor, and the calling out of the state militia. To compound the situation, the state was engaged in a bitter political battle between the Bourbon Democrats and the Populists. Alabama's organized labor movement was strongly Populist, so that the often cited lack of co-operation between union men and Populists did not hold true in Alabama.

9

Aside from the work of research, the writers' major difficulty has been to determine the proper approach to their subject. How can such a vital event as a strike involving 8,000 men be presented in academic terms? It would be inaccurate to present heroic union men battling against oppressive management made stronger by the support of state and local government. In point of fact, many of the strikers were heroic, but management should not be indicted as callous robber barons who delighted in watching miners and their families starve. Indeed, there have been few men more dynamic than Henry F. DeBardeleben, whose career merits a full scale biography. There is also need for an account of Governor Thomas G. Jones's two administrations. Whatever the shortcomings of this work, it is not intended to villify or glorify. Rather, the basic purpose has been to present events and interpret them from the viewpoint of prevailing conditions in the 1890's.

The authors owe a special debt of thanks to Milo Howard of the Alabama Department of Archives and History who provided valuable advice and generously made research material available. Also helpful were Professor Norman Pollack of Yale University, Dean Paul F. Carroll of Georgia Southern College, and Professor Thomas B. Alexander of the University of Alabama. Miss Leslie McNevin, a student at Florida State University, prepared the drawing designating the coal mines from which the final map was drawn. Grateful appreciation is extended to the Faculty Research Committee of Georgia Southern College and to the staffs of the following institutions: Alabama Department of Archives and History, Birmingham Public Library, University of Alabama Library, Georgia Southern College Library, and the Florida State University Library.

Statesboro, Georgia   *Robert David Ward*
Tallahassee, Florida   *William Warren Rogers*

Labor Revolt in Alabama

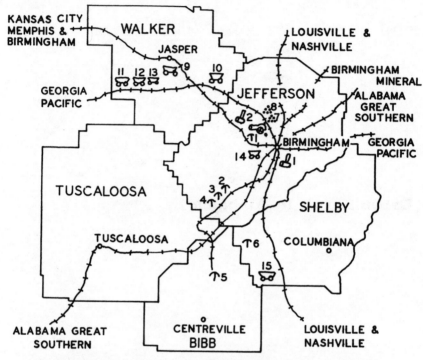

LOCALE OF ALABAMA'S LABOR DISTURBANCES IN 1894

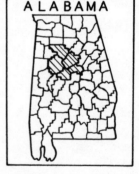

PROPERTIES OF THE TENNESSEE COAL,
IRON AND RAILROAD COMPANY:

1 PRATT	4 SUMTER
2 ADGER	5 BLOCTON
3 JOHNS	6 GURNEE

PROPERTIES OF SLOSS IRON & STEEL COMPANY:

7 BROOKSIDE 8 CARDIFF

OTHER MINES:

9 HEWITT	13 COAL VALLEY
10 CORDOVA	14 DOLOMITE
11 CORONA	15 MONTEVALLO
12 PATTON	

SITES OF UNION MEETINGS:

1 LAKEVIEW 2 ADAMSVILLE

CAMP FORNEY

chapter 1

Early Efforts at Organization

A violent and protracted strike began in Alabama coal mines on April 14, 1894. The strike involved more than 8,000 miners seeking to protect themselves against wage reductions in a time of depression, and hoping to gain peripheral improvements in living and working conditions. This strike, the largest demonstration by organized labor in the state during the nineteenth century, lasted through four violent months. In an era of industrial warfare the Alabama strike was a product of its time, a part of the struggle between management and labor that accompanied the post Civil War decades of industrialization. In many ways the Alabama strike shows the usual symptoms of the 1890's: clashes between strikers and company guards, the use of Pinkerton detectives, and the ultimate employment of the state militia to quell violence both real and potential. On these bases the Alabama strike would remain an isolated provincial example of labor unrest, overshadowed by the labor conflicts of the more industrialized North.

The Alabama coal mine strike, however, cannot be so easily categorized, for in several ways it was unique. The 1894 strike was fought out in a society still basically agrarian in its attitudes and its values, a society not yet fundamentally affected by the changes to be wrought by blast furnace and rolling mill. In such a setting the strike was alien, a foreshadowing of the future. It intruded on past and present in its use of the coercive power of the group in a society still operating on personal relationships. This was a Southern strike, and as such it transcended the accepted elements of industrial warfare. Here the difficulties of improved wages, better working conditions, and attempts at unionization were compounded by the convict lease system and volatile racial animosity. Here, in 1894, the political movement of agrarian reform joined with the cause of the proletariat to produce a turbulent upheaval.

The strike of 1894 was the product of its own peculiar genesis, half colored by national developments, half formed by its sectional setting. A background that requires consideration and understanding produced the four months of crisis.[1]

The coal fields of Alabama are divided geographically into three major segments. On a line running roughly from southeast to northwest through the center of the state lie the Coosa, the Cahaba, and the Warrior coal fields, each named for the river that drains these valley basins. Despite the extensive area underlaid by the coal measures, the commercial exploitation of coal has centered in a compact group of counties, notably in Jefferson, Walker, Bibb, Tuscaloosa, St. Clair, Shelby, and Talladega.[2]

While coal was mined in Bibb and Shelby counties as early as 1815, nothing approaching the status of a coal industry was discernible until the eve of the Civil War.[3] This relatively slow development of the state's extensive coal deposits was attributable in part to the basic capital deficiencies of the time, but even more to the fact that prior to the Civil War the limited utilization of Alabama iron ore was not dependent on coal. A charcoal-based iron process placed no premium on the large-scale mining of coal.

In 1856, "the first regular, systematic, underground mining" was begun near Montevallo in the Cahaba field by the Alabama Coal Mining Company.[4] In 1859, the company installed a steam engine for mine haulage, a technical improvement put to good use with the arrival of Joseph Squire, an English-born, practical mining engineer. At that time it cost the company $10.00 a ton to mine its coal. With the new equipment and better organization, Squire soon cut .this expense to $2.50 and at the same time raised the wages of his miners to $1.00 a ton.[5]

While the slow infiltration of technical advance and better management provided a basis for industry, it was the temporary stimulus of the Civil War and the demand for coal and iron by the Confederate government that brought rapid growth in production.[6] Though the Shelby Iron Company played an important role in supplying the Confederacy with critically needed iron, events soon showed that the demands of war were a transitory basis on which to found an industry. The Shelby works were destroyed by Union raiders in 1865; the end of the war brought a cessation of demand; the small operators drifted away; and the mine sites returned to the brier-ridden abandonment of a rugged country.

The resurrection of coal and iron production in Alabama was a hesitant part of the unprecedented national growth that followed the Civil War. With little native capital, inadequate transportation, and a host of technical unknowns, the exploitation of Alabama coal and iron nevertheless drew individuals willing to run the risks of the untried in hopes of profit to come. The creation of a relatively complex industrial economy in a war-impoverished agrarian society met with delay and frustration. The requirements of the retail market could support a few mines as a source of domestic fuel, but such demands were far too small to activate large-scale coal mining. Greater coal production could only come as a side effect of the development of an iron industry, and both were dependent on railroad building to open the mineral region to development. It was this interrelationship of need between coal, iron, and railroads that posed the major impediment to growth in the immediate postwar period. William Crawford Gorgas, former head of Confederate Ordnance, wrote, "the mining interest and the Rail Road interest must go hand in hand—the latter must lead the former & must then be sustained by it. . . ."[7] From 1866 to 1868 Gorgas tried but failed to produce iron profitably at the Brierfield Iron Works near Ashby, Alabama.[8]

Though slow at first, the industry's growth began even before the period of Reconstruction had run its course. In 1872 native capital was invested in a renewal of iron production when Daniel Pratt, Alabama's pioneer textile manufacturer, his son-in-law, Henry F. DeBardeleben, and Henry D. Clayton took over the prewar Oxmoor furnace under the name of the Eureka Mining Company.[9] The success of this venture perhaps seemed the more assured when in the same year the old South and North Railroad, authorized by the state in 1860, was finally completed under the ownership of the Louisville & Nashville Railroad. The road ran through the heart of the mineral region, but whatever dreams of profit the officers of the L. & N. may have had in controlling transportation from Nashville to Montgomery, they were long in realizing them. The Panic of 1873 found the L. & N. overextended and without credit. The extensive coal mines and iron works on which the route was premised did not yet exist, and the few that did offered scant traffic and less revenue. As the vice-president of the L. & N. morosely put it, the railroad "will not pay for the grease that is used on its car wheels."[10]

At the same time the Oxmoor experiment of the Eureka Mining Company was faring little better. Its furnaces went into blast in the early winter of 1873 in time to be hit by the panic that drove pig iron prices from $40.00 a ton to $8.00. DeBardeleben, who had been acting as general manager, resigned, and although the company was reorganized as the Eureka Mining and Transportation Company it remained short of capital and technically hindered because of its reliance on charcoal.

It was not until four years after the Panic of 1873 that the basic questions of Alabama's industrial future were answered. In 1876 it was demonstrated that good quality iron could be made with coke, a discovery that immediately produced the first systematic examination of the coal fields. The leaders in this exploration were Truman H. Aldrich, a trained mining engineer from New York who had bought the Montevallo mines in 1873; James W. Sloss, an interested party in the South and North Railroad and a member of the board of managers of the Eureka Company; and DeBardeleben, once more drawn into the business of coal and iron.[11]

In 1878 Aldrich, Sloss, and DeBardeleben formed the Pratt Coal and Coke Company and began major mining operations in the Pratt seam of the Warrior coal field. From this point onward the expansion of the coal industry was rapid because new capital flowed into the business and the consolidation of small companies began. Although opportunity for the small entrepreneur remained open for some time, high production costs caused a trend toward control of the industry by a few major companies. While concentration of management produced economics in operation and greater economic power for the owners, it also increased the effectiveness of labor pressure once the difficulties of union organization were overcome.

The Pratt Coal and Coke Company of Aldrich, Sloss, and DeBardeleben was itself the basis for further expansion and consolidation. In 1881 Aldrich left the company to organize his own larger Cahaba Coal Mining Company. In the same year Sloss resigned and organized the Sloss Furnace Company.

DeBardeleben, under the apparently erroneous assumption that he was suffering from tuberculosis, sold the Pratt Company to Tennessee interests headed by Enoch Ensley. Ensley, in 1884, combined his new property with the Alice Furnace Company and the Linn Iron Works to create the Pratt Coal and Iron Company.

The next round of organizational change carried concentration much farther. In 1886 the Pratt Coal and Iron Company was, in effect, bought out from under Ensley when majority control was acquired by the Tennessee Coal, Iron, and Railroad Company, up to now an exclusively Tennessee-based concern. In the same year DeBardeleben returned to the scene of action and established the DeBardeleben Coal and Iron Company. The ingredients were now in place for the major merger that came in 1891. In that year the Tennessee Company acquired not only DeBardeleben's large holdings, but took over the Cahaba Coal Mining Company of T. H. Aldrich as well. In 1892 the Tennessee Company elected new officers for its consolidated holdings, with Nat Baxter of the original company as president, DeBardeleben as first vice-president, and Aldrich as second vice-president and general manager.

Thus constituted, the Tennessee Company held the major portion of the coal business of the state.[12] It operated ten mines at its Pratt Mines Division, the heart of the old Aldrich, Sloss, and DeBardeleben company. In addition, its Blue Creek Division carried on operations at the major mines of Adger, Johns, and Sumter, and the Cahaba Division mined three slopes at Blocton and two at Gurnee. The closest competitor was the Sloss Iron and Steel Company, organized in 1887, with mines at Coalburg, Brookside, Cardiff, Brazil, and Blossburg.[13]

Company consolidation was a by-product of the basic enlargement of the industry that was taking place. From 13,000 tons of coal mined in the state in 1870, production rose to over 5,500,000 tons by 1892. Almost nine-tenths of the total production of the state was centered in the three counties of Jefferson, Walker, and Bibb, with Jefferson, the center of the iron industry, producing one-half of the total state production. The total value of the coal produced in 1892 was estimated at $5,788,898. In coal mining alone the New South's version of big business had arrived by 1892.[14]

Several cities were direct products of Alabama's coal and iron production, but Birmingham's growth was the most spectacular. In 1869 the coal, iron, and other mineral deposits around the small village of Elyton in Jefferson County were noted.[15] From this town and the surrounding area the city of Birmingham was to grow. By the spring of 1871 Col. J. R. Powell's land company had surveyed 300 acres of land, divided it into blocks, and subdivided these into lots, and was offering them for sale at prices ranging from $75 to $150. The South and North Railroad built a depot, and a local paper announced, "the prospects of Birmingham on the whole seem flattering."[16] That this was an understatement may be seen in the census returns for the next decades. In 1870 Jefferson County had 12,345 persons; by 1880 the population had grown to 23,272 and by 1890 to 88,501.[17] Birmingham itself increased from 3,086 persons in 1870 to 26,501 in 1890.[18] "The sky and the horizon were their limits, and they laid the foundations accordingly," an admiring chronicler wrote of the founders.[19] City tax values leaped from $2,500,000 to over $40,000,000 in the period from 1879 to 1887.[20] But, as the center of the state's industrial production, Birmingham also became the center of industrial strife and discord.

Coincident with enlarged production and the control of Alabama coal mining by a few companies, the labor force to be employed in mining was taking shape. It was the composition of this labor force that vitally affected both the movement for unionization and the difficulties facing unions in their use of the strike. By 1889, four groups comprised the mining labor

force of the state. Native-born whites made up 34.9 per cent of
the total. While many in this group were miners drawn in from
other states, it seems certain that most were native Alabamians,
still closely tied to their agrarian past.[21] The second group of
miners, 18.7 per cent, came from abroad, principally as immi-
grants from England, Scotland, and Ireland.[22] Many of the
early mines in Alabama were named for the nationalities of
these miners, as the ruins of the Irish Pit and the Dutch Pit
near Montevallo testify. The Dutch (probably Germans) are
reputed to have built their own brewery because of distaste for
the local product. Because their background and language were,
for the most part, similar to those of the native-born, this group
did not constitute a seriously divisive element in the labor force.

While Northern Europeans entered Alabama mining with a
minimum of friction, the Southern Europeans often met an
unyielding hostility. As early as 1879 an editor welcomed immi-
grant workers "provided you are not tramps, strikers, communists, nor Mollie Maguires. . . ."[23] In 1885, twenty-three Italians
were brought in by the management of the Warrior Coal Mines.
The Italians, either in festive or hostile mood, made a grand
entrance into town firing revolvers. The local miners, acting in
the belief that the Italians "were imported to reduce wages for
mining," were moved to counteraction.[24]

A committee representing 400 of the miners had the Italians
arrested on a charge of firing weapons, thus precipitating a local
debate on the question of importing foreign labor. The leader
of the local miners stated that "we do not intend to harm the
men who came here, but they are not going to take our places
in the mines. We came here first and propose to stay. It is no use
talking, it is our men or no other miners." These sentiments
were sharply attacked by a spokesman for property as an example of "mobocracy" when such men "presume to tell an intelligent community of business men that they propose to dictate
who a man may employ and who he shall not employ."[25] When

the Birmingham *Iron Age* defended employers in importing labor, it was rebuked by the Birmingham *Sunday Chronicle* on the grounds that "no foreign labor broker should be allowed to plant his transient colony in the state to absorb the wages that should belong to our citizens. . . ."[26]

If an incident such as this occasionally roiled the labor waters, the problem of foreign labor was not great enough to produce a major disturbance. Of far greater import and influence were the Negroes employed in coal mining. In 1889, 46.2 per cent of coal miners in the state were Negroes. While they did not outnumber the whites, they served as a bar to an effective labor movement and as a strikebreaking force always available to the coal mine operators.[27] Many Negroes were loyal supporters of unionization, but the use of Negro strikebreakers intensified existing racial bitterness and made the Negroes' role in the union movement eminently more difficult. Whatever the common economic interests shared by white and Negro miners, the labor force's mixture often tended to transcend and obscure the more immediate demands of labor solidarity.[28]

The white-Negro mixture in the labor force was not the only element affecting labor-management relations. To further complicate relationships there was the convict lease system of the state government and the employment given to convicts by the major coal companies. Union labor, white and black, competed against nonunion labor; white miners competed against Negro miners; and all groups of free miners were in competition with convict labor.

The convict lease system stands as an illustration of two cardinal points in the attitude of the conservative Democrats or Bourbons who gained control of Alabama government following Reconstruction. First, the system paid homage to the shibboleth of economy in government, and permitted the Bourbon Democrats to compare their frugality with the prodigality of Republican Reconstruction. In addition, convict leasing indicated a property alliance of big planter with business and industry. Convict leasing saved the state money while operating to the financial benefit of those who employed the convicts.

In January 1888, ten concerns made bids to the state for convict labor. An exclusive contract was given to the Tennessee Company for ten years on condition that the company take all convicts that were able to work. The company promised to recompense the state at a rate ranging from $9.00 to $18.00 a month, depending on the classification of the convict. When the other bidders protested the contract award, a legislative committee investigated. Although the legislative committee recommended canceling the contract, the governor did not do so because the company agreed to abide by the terms of the contract in the future. In addition to its state convicts, the Tennessee Company also worked county convicts, although it divided these with the Sloss Iron and Steel Company.

In 1894, the Tennessee Company had 1,138 convicts at its Pratt Mines prison, and was actually working 954 of these in the mines at an average annual cost of $108.13 per convict.[29] The Sloss Company at Coalburg had a total of 589 convicts, and was using 438 of them in mine operations. In total, 1,392 convicts were mining coal and performing labor that otherwise would have employed free miners.[30] This use of convict labor was a source of continued bitterness and agitation among the free miners. It operated both as a powerful impetus toward organization and a major issue in miner political orientation.

The early history of unionization and strike activity in Alabama coal mining is fragmentary in both chronology and detail. Enough evidence exists to demonstrate clearly the basic outlines of a rudimentary labor movement developing in an environment almost completely inimicable to successful union activity. As G. S. Mitchell points out, unionization was in general unimportant in the South before World War I, yet in the

mining industry the union movement had considerable importance even before 1900,[31] and miners made continued attempts
in the face of repeated failures.

The first of the coal mine strikes on record in Alabama occurred in March 1879, when miners struck the J. T. Pierce
Company and the Alabama Mining Company in protest of
wage reductions from $1.00 a ton to 80 cents a ton. Whether
the miners won this strike is unknown. If it followed later pat-
terns, it probably ended in failure.[32] No other strikes seem to
have occurred in 1879, although it is apparent that by this date
the problems of capital and labor were becoming matters of concern in Alabama. One newspaper, praising a recently organized Agricultural and Mechanical Association, observed that
the new group, "unlike the Grange," excited no "jealousy or
hostility,"[33] although in actual fact the Alabama Grange was a
rather conservative organization. Another newspaper condemned the speeches of a Greenback organizer for sowing discord between labor and capital. "What good are these
evangelists doing," argued the paper, "as they go from city to
city, using their utmost endeavors to enrage the people, and
bring about a bitter conflict between the necessary elements of
every prosperous country?"[34]

The motivation for stirring up discord between labor and
management was well demonstrated by the July 1880 strike
of miners at Coketon. The strikers protested a situation in
which they were forced to pay for the labor employed in push-
ing the tram cars from the main slope, and insisted that such
labor should be paid for by the company. The issue illustrates
the vagaries of the coal industry where miners, in effect, had
to pay to get the coal out of the mines. The company easily
broke the strike by moving more than 100 convicts into the
mines.[35]

Aside from his difficulties in trying to cope with the use of

convicts as strikebreakers, the Alabama miner's basic problem
was organization. In an economic and political situation where
the fulcrum of force lay so strongly with the operators, strikes
by single mines had little if any chance of success. An answer
to this problem began to appear during 1879-80 when the first
local assemblies of the Knights of Labor were organized at
Helena, Jefferson, Pratt, New Castle, and Warrior.[36] Membership in the local assemblies was secret, and the miners' wish for
secrecy has made the role of the Knights extremely difficult to
assess. Many of the strikes of the 1880's were probably inspired
by the Knights, although their passion for anonymity has left
the barest record of their activities.

A strike in May 1882, referred to by the local press as conducted by a "miners association," was definitely associated with
a Knights of Labor assembly. It involved over 500 miners at the
Pratt Mines striking in protest of a summer reduction in wages
from 50 cents a ton to 45 cents. After a strike of 31 days, during
which 200 convicts and perhaps 25 "blacklegs"—the standard
term among miners for strikebreakers—continued to work, the
wage dispute was compromised with the company granting a
summer rate of 47½ cents a ton.[37]

After a peaceful year in 1883, renewed labor activity took
place in 1884. On March 15, ninety-three miners at Coalburg
went on strike against a wage reduction. The strike was not
broken by the company until August 1, an exceptionally long
strike for this period. The company victory apparently hinged
on its importation of fifty blacklegs, and the miners were forced
to accept a cut in wages from $2.00 a day to $1.85.[38] The other
two coal mine strikes of 1884 were more successful. On May 1,
miners at Warrior, one of the mines where it is known that a
Knights of Labor council was organized, went on strike to prevent wage cuts, and on June 1, the company agreed to maintain
the scale at $1.75 a day.[39] Having won on the wage issue, the
Warrior miners immediately went on strike again in protest

against the hiring of foreign labor. By August 1, they had won
on this point as well, and the company stopped its importation.[40]

In the following year, the militant Warrior miners returned
to the charge with a strike on May 1, 1885, in an attempt to
gain semi-monthly payments. Losing in this attempt, the same
miners struck again in June against the company's renewed
attempt to import foreign laborers. This time the embattled
miners won their point.[41]

Other miners did not fare as well in 1885. One miner, protesting charges that union men had burned company property
at a mine at Stockton, argued that "the miners union [perhaps
a local Knights council] has no purpose or any feature connected with it which manufactures incendiaries or to do any
act of violence to company property. . . ." In bitter vein the
miner continued:

> The men who went in at the new company prices are not coal-
> diggers, and the operators will find it cheaper to have paid min-
> ers a living wage to dig their coal than have their mines butch-
> ered by those inexperienced men, and it is only a matter of time
> when they will have to pay a living price and all union men are
> satisfied of this.[42]

Miners realized that state convicts could be used as an effective strikebreaking force. Even without such use in strikes,
the miners had every reason to oppose convict leasing as a direct
impingement on free labor opportunity. During the 1880's the
convict question was a rallying point for miner organization,
less influential politically than during the 1890's, but effective
as a proving ground for miner co-operation in the face of a
common problem.

On July 18, 1885, miners met in Birmingham to organize
the Miners Anti-Convict League and Union of Alabama—"the
first effort toward making a systematic war on the use of con-

victs in competition with free labor in this state."[43] The new
league made a public declaration that:

> It is not beneficial to the state in any sense to take into her treas-
> ury the wages which should go into the pockets of free men, to
> be put in constant circulation. It is not well for great corpora-
> tions and a great state to use the criminal classes, to prevent free
> men from earning wages with which to buy homes, and support
> families. It is not right to fill the mines with convicts and crowd
> out free labor which could earn fair wages at this dangerous
> work.[44]

The League pledged that a "steady determination" would actu-
ate it in its efforts to abolish the convict lease system, and that
it would use "none but peaceful means" in its agitation.[45]

In August 1885, the League held another meeting to keep
the issue before the public. The Birmingham *Sunday Chronicle,*
favorable toward the miners' cause, went to some pains to deny
any radical intent on the part of the League. "Some even think,"
stated the paper, "that the League is a branch of the labor
unions organized to combat and terrify capital." The League
was no combination against capital; rather "it is a combination
of men of like interests to protect themselves against an offen-
sive and oppressive convict system. . . ."[46] The newspaper was
correct. The Anti-Convict League was not a labor union, although it did constitute a vital training ground for union organization yet to come.

After the strikes of 1884 and 1885, the following year was
one of deceptive quiet. While nationally the Knights of Labor
were carrying on their greatest strike activity against the Gould
railroad system, it is interesting to note that the Knights'
Birmingham organizer was quoted by the Birmingham *Sunday
Chronicle* on March 28, 1886, as declaring that the Knights
were not "Molly Maguires, nor communists, nor socialists. We

want no disorder, nor trouble nor strikes." This no-strike attitude was in keeping with the general philosophy of the national
leadership, but such a policy may have had little appeal for
hard-pressed miners. At any rate, 1886 marked the beginning
of Knight decline in Alabama coal mining. It was in this year
that the National Federation of Miners and Mine Laborers
was organized, and it immediately entered into an intense ri-
valry with the Knights for miner membership.[47]

Whether because of the activities of the Knights or the National Federation, an exceptionally large strike closed fourteen
mines in Walker County in February 1887. The 1,341 miners
who went on strike ignored the usual posture of defense against
wage reductions and demanded wage increases of 20 per cent.
The strike was broken in twenty-four days, but it marked a
strong advance over earlier single mine strikes that were limited
in the pressure they could bring to bear.[48] Strikes also occurred
at the Corona and Pratt mines in May, 1888. The Corona strike
involved wages and company store prices, and the miners won
some concessions on both scores. The Pratt strike apparently
ended in failure.[49]

Obviously motivated by organizational effort, miners met in
Birmingham in May 1888, in an attempt to formulate a uniform pay scale for mining. While a state pay scale might have
presupposed a state wide union already in existence, this convention first set up a temporary organization to guide its deliberations. The miners were prepared to tackle the questions of
a uniform scale and state organization simultaneously.[50]

Pursuing their task, the miners met again in Birmingham on
July 20, 1888. The question confronting the meeting was one
of basic policy. Should the miners create an independent state
miners' union or affiliate with the Knights of Labor, an order
declining in membership and power because of public disfavor
and organizational difficulties? The answer given at the meeting

proved that the Knights had lost the trust and allegiance of the majority of the rank and file. A state federation of miners received a vote of 1,335, while affiliation with the Knights was backed by only 310 of those present.[51] No official name was given to this newly-created union, and it is as hard to correlate strike activity with this group as to correlate it with the Knights.

It is plain, however, that following the establishment of the Miners' Federation, strike activity began to be manifested in concentrated fashion. In October 1888, miners at Blocton struck against a reduction in wages, and in the same month Pratt miners walked out (answering an organization call) in protest against a 10 per cent wage cut. In November yet another strike occurred in Walker County in an attempt to half wage reductions.[52] All three strikes ended in failure.

The upswing in labor unrest continued in 1889. In May, 525 miners struck in Birmingham against a reduction in wages of 25 per cent. In June, 281 miners at Corona attempted to stop a wage cut of 10 per cent, while in October miners at Coalburg were protesting wage decreases of 9.0 per cent.[53]

This long catalogue of seldom-relieved failure is at least instructive on the difficulties that confronted Alabama miners. Even in situations where organization was strong enough to bring about county-wide strikes, the miners' endurance was extremely short. Strikes in the summer months, when the demand for mine labor was low, diluted the economic pressure the miners could exercise. Winter strikes, conducted with totally inadequate treasuries and little outside strike relief, were almost always doomed to failure by the miners' marginal personal finances.

The easy recruitment of non-union labor by the mine operators, plus the unprepossessing record of early strike activity undoubtedly influenced many miners to think that unionization was futile. If the Knights of Labor had failed to achieve a strongly unified miners' union in the state during the 1880's, the organization of the independent state federation at the close of the decade at least showed a rising spirit of labor consciousness. These were the educational years for Alabama miners, as they were for the national labor movement. They had not yet learned all their lessons, but they had become infinitely more experienced than in their opening strikes of 1879.

chapter 2

Unionization, Political Revolt and Panic

As the decade of the 1890's opened, Alabama miners had few material gains to show for over ten years of labor agitation. A state miners' organization had been created in 1888, but it had failed to prove itself an effective agent of the miners' interests. Wages had not greatly improved, and convict labor still toiled in the mines.

In the new decade the old problems and antagonisms were to be sharpened and intensified by depression and unemployment. Hard times increased labor militancy, while farmer-labor political revolt shook the foundations of the ruling order. Feeding on the reform movements of the agrarians, the miners of Alabama became more organized and far more active than they had even been before. The recognition and outright avowal of economic and class interests, stifled in Alabama by the rationalizations of the Bourbon order, were slow in developing but the more devastating on their final arrival.

After years of organizing attempts by Alabama miners, it was a national event that seemed to offer coherence and a sense of direction to the local effort. On January 25, 1890, the United Mine Workers of America was organized at Columbus, Ohio. Although no Alabama miner sat in this first convention, Alabama was accorded membership as a part of District 20.[1] The creation of the national UMW afforded a strong rallying point for Alabama miners and offered an appeal for national affiliation surpassing the diluted attraction of the Knights of Labor.

In May 1890, the Miners' Trades Council, a Birmingham or Jefferson County organization, addressed itself to the problem of national affiliation. With some degree of unanimity the Council declared itself "heartily in favor of organizing the district and immediately connecting . . . with the United Mine Workers of America."[2] Once the basic decision was made, the Council instructed its secretary to ask the national union for an organizer, and pending such an appointment, named its president, J. L. Conley of Blue Creek, to take up the work of unionization.[3] Conley worked with vigor, and by the end of June, local unions had been organized in Bibb, Jefferson, and Shelby counties. The Pratt Mines of the Tennessee Company had been organized, and the major holdings of the Sloss Iron and Steel Company at Cardiff, Blossburg, and Brookside were under organizational attack.[4]

On July 1, the Alabama leaders of the UMW, emboldened by the success of their organizing efforts, invited the mine operators to meet with them to discuss the adoption of the new national wage scale. The union called for an increase of 5 cents a ton and for maintaining the scale regardless of fluctuations in iron prices. On the appointed day the union officials assembled at the Pratt Mines. They were fortified by the presence of P. McBride of Pennsylvania, a member of the national UMW executive board, who not only attended this meeting but lent a hand in organizing by speaking at various mines. The meeting demonstrated, however, that to demand union recognition as a bargaining agent was altogether different from receiving it. While a few small operators attended the meeting, it was ignored by the major coal companies. In some bitterness the Birmingham *Labor Advocate* summed up the outcome: ". . . the great coal barons of the city held the wage earners in such perfect contempt that their request was almost wholly ignored, and it was therefore impossible to take any action of mutual interest. . . ."[5]

If the union was powerless to force its recognition on the companies, it could show its displeasure. Beginning on the abortive meeting day, 1,354 laborers at the Pratt Mines staged a four day strike of retaliation and warning.[6] Though the strike was officially reported as one called to gain a wage increase of 10 per cent, its short duration indicates that its real purpose was protest. The UMW's organizing success can be roughly calculated from the fact that of a total employment of 1,862 at the Pratt Mines, 1,354 miners struck. The situation now confronting the union left it with few alternatives. Only success could create the appeal that it needed for existence, and success required that the operators accept the demand for a 5 cents a ton wage increase. In early November the Pratt miners again met to discuss the wage issue, and their decision was for mass action.[7] On November 29, 1890, 3,417 miners, the largest number yet to participate in an Alabama strike, stopped work in a demand for the 5 cents a ton increase.

The strike was well-timed. In late November coal demand was at its yearly peak, and enough mines and miners were involved to lower coal production. By early January 1891, Mobile was almost out of coal. Some Alabama railroads were so short they were confiscating for their own use coal shipped on their lines.[8] But at the same time, the average price of coal fell from $1.10 per ton in 1889 to $1.03 in 1890,[9] and this alone would have made Alabama operators unreceptive to demands for a wage increase.

Once the strike was joined the initiative shifted to the coal companies, and vigorous counteraction was undertaken to break the strike and the union that had called it. Striking miners were evicted from company houses and property by armed guards; Negro strikebreakers were brought into the mines and paid bonuses; and the pro-company press of Birmingham attempted to capture public opinion and cast doubts on the miners' motives.[10] While the Birmingham *Labor Advocate* spoke out for the miners' cause, and the Birmingham Trades Council gave the strike its moral support, the *Age-Herald* and *Evening News,* the largest papers of the Birmingham area, reported that the strike had been broken. The presence on the scene of William Scaife, a member of the national UMW Executive Board, was interpreted as a plot by Pittsburgh coal dealers to foment a strike in Alabama in order to advance Pittsburgh at the expense of Birmingham. It was an uneven fight both journalistically and economically.[11] (The editor of the *Labor Advocate* complained on January 24, 1891, that the miners had not given him the necessary information so that he could accurately portray their cause to the public.) By January 13, 1891, the strike was broken. No increase in wages had been won, and some miners were fired for union activity.[12] In its initial trial of strength, the Alabama UMW had failed. It did not get a second chance.

On January 20, 1891, the United Mine Workers held its state convention in Birmingham. The convention condemned the Birmingham *Age-Herald* and *Evening News* for "having placed themselves in a position at once antagonistic to the cause of organized labor and to the common interests of the great mass of the common people of Alabama. . . ."[13] With empty defiance the delegates expressed themselves in favor of a wage scale of

50 cents a ton, although there was no hint of another strike to make the demand a reality.

When President Conley attended the first annual convention of the national UMW in February 1891, he already represented a crumbling organization. The national convention's donation of $500 to help the "downtrodden" Alabama miners was no reviving force against the crushing defeat of the strike.[14] With increasing rapidity the Alabama UMW moved from substance to shadow and into oblivion. It disappeared almost as completely as if it had never been organized in the state.[15]

A two year period of quiescence in the mining industry followed. While the UMW had been destroyed by the complete failure of its strike attempt, the return of better times during 1891 and 1892 made further efforts at unionization less imperative. Coal prices moved upward to $1.07 a ton, and production and the number of miners increased, though there is no evidence that wages did the same.[16] In vain the Birmingham *Labor Advocate* admonished the miners to reaffiliate with the national UMW: ". . . you may have no need of organization now, but some day you may, and we would have you remember that thorough preparation is half the battle."[17]

If a limited and relative prosperity dimmed the miners' interest in union organization, some steps of lasting significance to the labor movement did occur. The early difficulties of the Alabama labor movement had been reflected and accentuated by the problems of establishing a labor press in the state. Only a sympathetic press could provide the leadership and furnish the educational background for economic class consciousness. In 1886, Captain George N. Edwards published the *Labor Union* in Birmingham. Edwards' intent was to advocate policies "believed . . . best promotive of the rights and interests of labor."[18] The first issue of the *Labor Union* was to appear on April 24, 1886, with a run of 4,000 copies for distribution among the working class. But Edwards' venture ended in failure (perhaps his position as Commander of the Grand Army of the Republic in Alabama contributed to the paper's demise),[19] and the *Labor Union* was succeeded in 1887 by the *Alabama Sentinel,* the official organ of the Knights of Labor. The *Sentinel* was an effective voice for labor and reform, but the decline of the Knights diminished the influence of its newspaper.[20]

Easily the most influential champion of the workingman's rights was the Birmingham *Labor Advocate,* published and edited by Jere Dennis.[21] The editor brought to his new task a background of newspaper experience which included work on the Dadeville *Star,* and an apparently strongly-developed social conscience. Dennis' explanation for his journalistic venture was imbued with strong overtones of the class struggle:

> We suppose you would like to know our reasons for starting a paper, particularly a *Labor Advocate.* Well, have you spent fifteen years of your life tramping around over the world setting type for someone else? Have you ever been a day laborer and been imposed upon when you were powerless and helpless by those who would not dare look you in the face when your hands were untied?[22]

Dennis became a central figure in Birmingham labor circles. He sat on the Birmingham Trades Council as a representative of the Typographical Union. In January 1890, his first month as editor of the *Labor Advocate,* he was appointed general organizer for the American Federation of Labor for the Birmingham district.[23]

Although a large part of the *Labor Advocate* was devoted to boilerplate materials, Dennis hammered home the theme of organization as the only hope of the workingman. His reform interests were catholic, and he pushed the activities of the Farmers' Alliance, the Knights, and the Greenbackers with equal impartiality. Dennis' readers were constantly reminded that the bulk of society labored under the injustices of a greedy

ruling order of special interest, ever awake to exploit and im-
poverish the toilers of the land. "The poor man," wrote Dennis,
"is called a socialist if he believes that the wealth of the rich
should be divided among the poor, but the rich man is called
a financier if he devises a plan by which the pittance of the poor
can be converted to his use."[24] His materials came from a central agency such as the National Reform Press Association.
Every issue of the *Advocate* carried a column headed "Alliance
Reading—Matters of Importance to the Order and to Those
Who Believe in its Teachings." Though his strictures on the
rich and his calls for action by the oppressed were exaggerated,
his influence was considerable.

Alabama coal miners, and other segments of labor in the
state as well, did not struggle in isolation nor live in a vacuum.
Their attempts to unionize were part and parcel of the total
milieu. Both industrial laborers and farmers were gradually
coming to realize the strong connection between economics and
politics and were increasingly aware that political activity was
the best route to their desired economic goal. But their way
was blocked by the powerful coalition between planter and in-
dustrialist which held political control of the state.

With the downfall of the Reconstruction government, political leadership had been seized by the planter and professional
classes in the Black Belt, the so-called Bourbon Democrats. Republican extravagances brought a reaction of strict govern-
mental economy and any inroads on the policy were extremely
slow. Yet in the 1880's as Alabama began to stir industrially
and as business became an important part of the state's economy, an accommodation between planter and industrial desires
had to be reached, and despite many obstacles, a political
alliance between large landholders and industrialists was
achieved.[25] There were charges that the coalition was based on
appeals to white supremacy rather than real issues. Later, there
would be charges of fraud and vote manipulation in the Black

Belt, where Negroes constituted a majority of the population. The alliance thrived nonetheless.

The reform movement in Alabama was both labor and agrarian in its inspiration. The agricultural distress of the small farmer that helped to fan his dissatisfaction with the status quo was echoed by the conditions of Alabama labor. Both groups believed they were the exploited of society; both came to feel themselves oppressed by the ruling order. Both the labor and agrarian aspects of the reform movement in Alabama fed strongly on outside sources of agitation and discontent, but conditions within Alabama gave them substance.

Almost from the beginning of reform agitation, the solidarity between agrarian and labor groups was apparent. In 1887 an attempt was made to form an Alabama Union Labor Party, affiliated with the National Union Labor Party organized in Cincinnati, Ohio, in the same year. The leader of this organizational effort was J. J. "Jonce" Woodall of Morgan County, an old Independent and Greenbacker, and secretary of the Morgan County Agricultural Wheel.[26] In September 1887, Woodall and others met in Birmingham to found their new party. About 100 delegates were present at the meeting; one-third of these were members of the Wheel, while the other delegates represented local unions and the Knights of Labor. The National Union Labor Party platform was adopted, and J. J. Jefferies of the Knights of Labor was elected permanent chairman. The meeting condemned national banks and the convict lease system, and voted to maintain a permanent state organization.[27]

The attempt to found the Union Labor Party in Alabama proved abortive, but its portent of challenge to the ruling order was not overlooked by the Montgomery *Advertiser,* the spokesman for and oracle of Bourbon Democracy. According to the paper, the Birmingham convention was attended by the "scum of creation . . . , anarchists, socialists and communists."[28]

While the Union Labor Party attempt offered no serious

threat to Bourbon supremacy, it was not an isolated event on the Alabama political scene. The very next year, 1888, a further effort at combined farmer-labor political action was made. This time the Knights of Labor took the lead in organizational effort. In March 1888, a meeting was called by the Knights of Labor "to devise a platform on which all laboring men could stand."[29] The meeting was attended by sixty-five or seventy delegates, representing the Knights of Labor, the Wheel, the Farmers' Alliance, the Tailors' Union, the Typographical Union, and the Carpenters' Union. At least one-third of the delegates were Negroes, and they were accorded representation on the various committees that were established. The meeting formally established the Labor Party of Alabama, and a platform was drawn up advocating better pay and working conditions, government ownership of the means of communication and transportation, better election laws, and a revision of the convict system.[30]

The Labor Party's rapid dissolution is a clear indication that organized labor in the state was neither influential nor numerous enough to constitute the hard core of political activity. The role of leadership now shifted to the agrarian organizations, the Agricultural Wheel and the Farmers' Alliance.

The Agricultural Wheel had been established in Alabama in 1886. Almost from its beginnings the organization indulged in fratricidal conflict between those who desired political activity and those who wished to steer clear of partisan involvement. The views of the former group were well summed up in a resolution passed by a local Wheel:

> We think the time has come for the laboring classes to lay down all political prejudices and rise above lines, and demand of our representatives a strict account of their political actions, and when they refuse to work for the interest of the masses, we deem it our duty to keep them at home, and send men there to represent us who will not violate their pledges.[31]

These were not the views of a majority of the members, for in 1888 the Wheel passed resolutions specifically aimed at any attempt at political activity by its members. The order's official newspaper, the *State Wheel,* was prohibited from advocating any party or endorsing any candidate.[32] The triumph of the nonpolitical faction of the Wheel was short-lived. The organization amalgamated with the more powerful Farmer's Alliance in 1889 and lost its identity at this point.

The major attempt at agrarian reform in Alabama centered in the Farmer's Alliance, first organized in the state in 1887. For the first three years of its existence, the Alliance concentrated on educational work among the farmers, and attempted to alleviate agricultural distress through self-help activities of co-operative buying and Alliance sponsored business.[33] Not until 1890 and the failure of many Alliance business ventures did the order turn massively to political action. Such action had been foreshadowed almost from the time of its organization. In 1889 there was much speculation concerning a union between the Knights of Labor and the Alliance. Most Alliance members were still too strongly embued with the ideology of conservative Democracy to view such a union with equanimity. The conservative Montgomery *Alliance Journal* spoke of the Knights as "the worst element of our population," bent on destroying all ownership of land.[34] The reform spirit of the Alliance was still in embryo.

As the Alliance became increasingly politically oriented after 1890, it came directly into conflict with the ruling group of the Democratic Party. The Bourbons attacked the political possibilities inherent in the farmers' movement, charging that white man's dissidence would endanger white supremacy. The *Alabama Sentinel,* official organ of the Knights of Labor, was quick to point out that "the Bourbon Democracy are trying to down the Alliance with the old cry 'nigger.' It won't work though."[35]

The first Alliance attempt at politics was to gain control of the Democratic Party. Farmers began to realize that they constituted the majority of the party's votes and that capturing the party from the inside would side-step the Bourbon charge that white supremacy was in danger. This strategy culminated in the unofficial Alliance endorsement of Eufaula's Reuben F. Kolb, the state commissioner of agriculture and a leader in the Alliance, for the governorship in 1890.[36]

In the state convention in May 1890, the contest was between Kolb and Thomas Goode Jones, the final choice of the "Stop-Kolb" forces. Since Jones later became the champion of the Bourbons, it is ironic that he was actually the weakest in the anti-Kolb camp. Jones' crities asserted that he owed his nomination to his inability to control his own delegates; the other candidates had to rally to him because he could not carry votes to any compromise candidate.[37] When Jones won nomination by the convention, Kolb made a conciliatory speech and pledged his support to the Democratic Party. Alliance strength was not yet directed on a path of political independence, but many of the order's members believed Kolb had been maneuvered out of the nomination by extra-legal methods.

Governor Jones was a Confederate veteran with an excellent war record who had continued his interest in military affairs after the war. He served with ability as colonel of the Alabama Militia from 1880 to his election as governor in 1890. By tradition and inclination a conservative, in the election he had the support of the state's major newspapers, most notably the powerful Montgomery *Advertiser*.

Jones's first two year term of office was a difficult one. He was viewed with suspicion by most Alliance men, who felt that Kolb should have been governor. Farmer animosity was increased when he vetoed a bill appropriating Hatch Act funds to the agricultural experiment station, and intensified yet more when he failed to reappoint Kolb as commissioner of agriculture.[38]

Although agrarian elements tested the policies of the Jones Administration and found them wanting, the mine workers were not led to a similar reaction at this time. During 1891 Jones was faced with the selection of a state mine inspector. The Tennessee Company advanced the candidacy of one of its officials named Riley. Peter Findlay and John DeB. Hooper, associated with small independent mines, were also advanced for the position. On March 8, 1891, John Harkins, secretary of the almost defunct United Mine Workers of America in Alabama, wrote Jones and urged Findlay's appointment, with Hooper as second choice. On March 16, Harkins returned to the issue and informed the governor that the "mine workers are unalterably opposed to an official of the Tennessee Coal and Iron Company receiving the appointment. . . ."[39] These sentiments were reiterated by a miner and former member of the Knights of Labor, who argued that the Tennessee Company had opposed the passage of a mine inspection law. This miner observed that the company worked "a very large number of convicts and have great power and influence"; if Riley of the Tennessee Company got the appointment "we had as well have no law."[40] Jones antagonized few of the miner rank and file when he appointed Hooper to the mine inspectorship.

Due to the vagaries of Alabama politics, Jones was little more than elected when he had to return to political campaigning. In December 1891, counties began to choose their delegates to the next state convention that would meet in June 1892. One of the first counties to act in the process was Jefferson, the largest of the mining counties. The results of the Jefferson primary offered evidence of strong Kolb strength but certainly failed to demonstrate that the miners had completely gone over to the cause of reform. Kolb and Jones actively campaigned in the county, and Jones received a plurality of the popular vote. As a result Jefferson's vote in the state convention was apportioned fourteen for Jones and twelve for Kolb.[41]

The delegate fight in Jefferson was viewed as a surprising and unexpected show of Kolb strength. One newspaper attributed Kolb's votes to "rash promises in regard to the convicts who are worked in Jefferson County, and with whom free labor have to compete."[42] It may be true that Kolb gained many miner votes, but at this time the miners were at their nadir of organizational woes. The election came at a time of labor peace, and prior to the Panic of 1893 that saw the intensification of miner economic distress and the resurgence of miner organization. .

L. W. Johns, superintendent of the DeBardeleben Coal and Iron Company, no doubt spoke for many conservatives when he congratulated Jones on his Jefferson County victory. According to Johns, "our boys at the mines . . . are highly elated over having come out on top, for they feel that good and honest government will prevail again for the next two years. . . ."[43] If there was evidence that some of the miners had supported Jones, there was also evidence that other miners along with many railroad employees had voted for Kolb.[44]

As the county contests for delegates continued throughout the state, there were sharpening portents of political revolution. In February 1892, a People's Party was formally established by Alliance members tired of equivocation and attempts to work within the Democratic Party. The leader of this third party movement, Joseph C. Manning, better known as "The Evangel," stated: "The People's Party is on a great boom. We have educated the farmers up to it, and we now propose to go to work on the laboring man. And we are going to get them."[45] It is significant that the powerful Jefferson County Alliance was among the first in the state to endorse the People's Party.[46] Despite unceasing efforts to convert the Alliance to open support of the People's Party, the rank and file of Alliance members were still unprepared for third party action.

During the political battles of the early spring, it became increasingly obvious that Kolb had little chance to win the nomination as a regular Democrat. Even in counties where

Kolb gained a majority of the delegates, Jones's supporters named rival slates. In a convention controlled by the regulars there was little doubt of the outcome on contested delegations.[47] Kolb privately announced that if Democratic injustices and fraud continued, "such a course will force two state conventions and two—nominations—I will be the nominee of the simon pure Jeffersonian Democrats, and Jones the nominee of the machine Democracy. . . ."[48] In May, Kolb openly announced his intentions of seeking the nomination as a Jeffersonian Democrat, arguing that the Jeffersonians would represent the true Democratic Party.[49]

Prior to the meeting of the state convention on June 8, Kolb supporters had already laid their plans for a separate convention and for a party organization in every congressional district. As peace overtures, the Kolbites first requested that Kolb delegates from forty-eight counties be seated in the state convention, a step which would have given Kolb the nomination. A second request was that Jones and Kolb face each other in a state-wide primary election for the nomination. When these proposals were turned down by the state executive committee, the Kolb forces held their own convention on the night of June 8, and nominated Kolb for the governorship.[50] When the regular convention nominated Jones, the Jeffersonians then held a further meeting to adopt a platform.

The platform of the Jeffersonian Democrats was a reform document of its times. It proposed a liberal public school system, and an equitable system of taxation; it opposed trusts and monopolies, called for the abolition of national banks and expansion of the currency to not less than $50.00 per capita, demanded the free and unlimited coinage of silver, and asked for a graduated federal income tax. Where the regular Democrats took the position that voting should be limited to the "intelligent and virtuous,"—a position that by implication called for the removal of the Negro from political life,—the Jeffersonians flatly stated that "we favor the protection of the colored race in their political rights. . . ." But these platform statements fail to explain party position. The majority of "Jeffersonian Democrats and regular Democrats did not feel that permitting Negroes to vote was a threat to white supremacy. The real question was *how* the Negro voted."[51] All in all, the platform of the Jeffersonian Democrats was far more a general platform of reform than a bill of particulars for the advancement of specific agrarian interests. Other than a demand for a reform of the state's election laws, it was at its more topical when it called for the prohibition of competition between convict and free labor.[52] Here was an outright appeal for the miners' votes.

The rancorous and vituperative campaign of 1892 between Jones and Kolb well illustrates the economic conflict of the times. The regular Democrats fought the Jeffersonians not simply to maintain their political power, but also to put down a movement that spoke for interests and classes hostile to Bourbon economic policies. Throughout the conflict the Bourbon forces campaigned vigorously to defeat what they regarded as a radical and subversive attack on the status quo. When the state elections were held in August, Jones was the victor with a majority of 11,435 votes out of a total of 243,037. The election was marked and marred by fraud so obviously conducted that even a Jones supporter could write his governor that "the only question is, what proportion will endorse it?"[53] There was, however, never the slightest suggestion that Governor Jones condoned any illegal practices.

Angered and embittered, Jeffersonians contended that fraudulent manipulation of the Negro vote in the Black Belt counties cost them the election. They vowed to continue the fight for Kolb's vindication and the triumph of Jeffersonian principles. But Bourbon control of the state administration was assured for two more years. Henry F. DeBardeleben of the Tennessee Company wrote Jones that "it is of great importance to the business men of the state to have you elected."[54] In like manner, Milton H. Smith, president of the Louisville and Nashville Railroad, pointed out to the governor that his tenure of office would benefit the people of Albama, "and the interests of the Louisville and Nashville R'd Co., as well as other companies operating railroads in the state, [will] be benefitted [sic]."[55]

The election of 1892 drew the lines of economic interest more explicitly than ever before. As the spokesman of farmers and a growing number of laborers, mine workers, and industrial employees, Kolb effectively dramatized a basic need for economic and political reform. In his second term Jones faced an increasingly bitter conflict between large planters and business interests on the one hand and small farmers and labor on the other. As the gulf between the two groups widened, mutual intransigence drove the reformers to acrimonious attacks while intensifying conservative determination against compromise or accommodation.

In the last months of 1892 it appeared that Governor Jones might lessen the antipathy of the Alabama coal miners. In Tennessee, coal miners had attacked the convict stockades in direct action.[56] Perhaps concerned that a similar resort to force might take place in Alabama, Jones congratulated the state's miners in November for not violently agitating the question of convict labor and gave his support to the report of his Convict Commission, which recommended that convicts be removed from the mines as soon as prison facilities could be made available. The governor showed understanding and even sympathy for the miners' opposition to convict labor.[57] But whatever promises he might hold out to the miners were more than offset by the polarization of political attitudes that had already taken place. To most of the miners Jones represented the enemy. They looked on him as the spokesman for the ruling group that had originally sent the convicts into the mines and believed his sympathies were with the companies that had profited from convict labor.

Increasingly during 1893 and 1894 the miners raised the issue of convict labor. This controversy was sharpened by the political agitation of the day and the worsening economic conditions miners began to face. On February 2, 1893, at Pratt City a mass meeting of miners culminated in a resolution asking for the immediate removal of the convicts from the mines.[58] "Pendragon," the Birmingham *Labor Advocate's* regular correspondent from the mines at Adger, argued the evils of convict labor, and pointedly reminded his fellow miners that "under no pretext whatever must the convicts compete with free labor after the next legislature has adjourned. The convicts must go."[59] One miner of mathematical bent analyzed convict labor on a hard economic basis. Assuming the employment of 1,600 convicts (there were actually 1,392 convicts mining coal in 1894), he computed convict production at about 96,000 tons per month:

> Then pay the Pratt mine convicts 45 cents per ton for their prorata of the 96,000 tons which would be 60,000 tons per month and multiply by 55 cents for Coalburg and 45 cents for Pratt Mines, and you have $43,500 in cash that has not become a circulating medium, and for one year $522,000 . . . that has gone into the pockets of three or four vaults, one the State, next the two mining corporation . . . , and the free men of the different branches of productive industry, and the merchants outside of the company 'pluck me stores' are deprived of the benefits of this labor.[60]

Writing in time of depression the analyst concluded that if free labor had gained this money in wages there would not have "been such a depression of times in Alabama as there has been." The farmer as well as the miner was hurt by the siphoning off of wages to the convicts, and both should make common cause by voting the same ticket.[61]

By 1894 if any miner doubted which political party served his interests, his doubts were dispelled by high authority. J. R. Sovereign, Master Workman of the Knights of Labor, spoke in Birmingham under the auspices of the Jeffersonian Democrats. Sovereign called for political action on the part of labor, and on the convict issue he stated, "I am glad there are candidates pledged to the removal of this curse from Alabama."[62]

A growing political consciousness suffused the ranks of Alabama labor, but the workers did not forget the primacy of their economic situation. The Alabama miners had long known economic hardship: low wages, long hours of work, debt, and grinding poverty. Economic distress had been the hard motive force for unionization; it was intensified by a depression that brought new attempts to organize out of the ashes of past failures. In 1893 the relative labor peace in the Alabama coal industry was shattered by economic recession. The Panic of 1893 had opened the door to the most concerted labor effort of the decade, and it dramatized in clear and unequivocal terms the political reformers' generalizations of exploitation and class interests. It is true, of course, that the coal companies were not impersonal giants presided over by men whose basic motive was greed. Economic recession hit management as well as labor. It would be the mode of response which would touch off conflict between the two.

The Panic, with rapid chain reaction, struck the mining industry when national demand for coal and iron began to fall. With the decline in iron prices and the slackening of demand, Alabama iron producers began to curtail production. This immediately affected the coal market, and the operators began the the process of trying to equate coal production with the lower level of demand. In 1893, 7.0 per cent fewer tons of coal were mined in the state than in 1892, while the value of the product declined by 12 per cent.[63] According to C. Vann Woodward, the year brought home "to the cities and industrial towns of

the South as never before the distress that had gripped the surrounding countryside for years."[64]

By May 1893, the Panic had manifested itself in business
failures and an increase in unemployment. In June, talk of
wage reductions was in the Alabama air, and rumors of reductions were closely followed by rumors of impending strikes.
The Birmingham *Age-Herald,* partial to the interests of the
coal and iron companies, spread the word that over 1,000 Negro
miners in Pennsylvania had made application to work in Alabama if the Alabama miners decided to strike. The paper argued
that Alabama miners were well paid and were working steadily.
Moreover, there was little for the miners to win and everything
to be lost if they struck. The *Labor Advocate* was as little pleased
with the situation, though for different reasons. As depression
overtook the industry the miners weree without effective organization. Editor Dennis lamented the miners' disorganization
and the fact that they "displayed nothing but suspicion and dis-
trust and indifference for their labor papers, labor leaders and
their own selves."[65]

The coal companies, finding their solvency in jeopardy, were
faced with alternatives of reaction. Their own stability could
be maintained either by laying off unneeded miners or maintaining employment levels but reducing the number of working days. Whichever alternative was taken, reducing wages
would be necessary to compensate for falling coal prices. As the
Panic made itself felt, a peculiar combination of policies was
actually followed. Working time decreased from an average of
271 days in 1892 to 237 in 1893, but employment increased
from 10,075 to 11,294. This additional employment in a time
when production was being reduced intensified the miners' belief that the companies deliberately attempted to reduce them
to a bare subsistence level.[66]

It was the giant of the Alabama coal industry, the Tennessee
Company, that made the first move to adjust to the Panic. The

Tennessee Company, long used to living on Wall Street credit, found itself with notes falling due and thousands of tons of pig iron that it could not sell.[67] The company announced a 10 per cent reduction in wages, and the first blow of the depression had now fallen on the miners' shoulders. On June 11, 732 miners of the Tennessee Company went on strike. The wage cut demanded by the company would have reduced the current 45 cents a ton to 40 cents, and the miners chose to combat the reduction eveen though job security was at a low ebb.[68]

The outcome of the miners' strike against the Tennessee Company affected the entire coal district. The Tennessee Company was the pacesetter in wage level determinations, and if the company succeeded in its 10 per cent reduction the smaller producers were sure to follow suit. By the end of June reports were heard that the other coal companies had already informed their men of wage cuts of five cents a ton. While this established a perfect basis for a general strike by all affected miners, there was no state-wide organization that could give direction and coordination in the crisis.[69] The battle would be fought on a company to company basis.

While the strike of the Pratt miners was not of long duration, it was filled with tension that moved from the coal fields to the state capital. With fears generated by the political agitation of the day, rumors spread that the striking miners intended to free the convicts at the mines and burn the stockades. While Governor Jones discounted the rumors, and publicly stated his confidence that the miners would not resort to lawlessness, he took steps to stop any effort against the convicts and protect the property of the coal companies. On June 22, the governor wrote to Milton H. Smith, president of the Louisville & Nashville Railroad, to ask if transportation could be furnished for state troops in the event of an outbreak by the miners. Smith responded that instructions had been issued "to furnish you all the transportation you may desire," though he hoped that "all

trouble with the miners will be avoided."[70] Jones was a vigorous
advocate of keeping the state troops well trained and ready for
action. Earlier in the year he had gained an appropriation of
$11,500 for encampments for the state troops, and somewhat
later, in October, he actually sent them into the Louisville and
Nashville shops at New Decatur. He was to call upon Smith
again to furnish transportation, but in 1893 he did not, at least,
use troops against the miners.[71]

Throughout the strike, the Pratt miners continued settlement conversations with company officials. The company argued
that if the miners accepted the wage reduction, two more furnaces could be built and the demand for coal increased. Labor
spokesmen claimed that the company could not solve its overproduction by building more furnaces, and urged the miners
to pay little attention to the argument.[72]

On July 1, a meeting of delegates from all the Tennessee
Company mines convened in Bessemer and decided to listen to
the company proposition. George B. McCormack, the assistant
general manager, spoke to the delegates, and it was apparent
that the company was willing to modify its original order for a
10 per cent reduction. The meeting's committee on scale made
its report for a "live and let live" policy with the company. The
committee suggested the maintenance of the 45 cents a ton scale
for the mines at Pratt and Blue Creek, and a four month reduction to 43 cents a ton at Blocton and Gurnee. During the
four months of reduction at the latter mines the company was
to reduce the price of powder and fuses. McCormack returned
to the meeting and the committee's report was handed to him
for company refusal or acceptance. After conferring with other
officials, McCormack announced that the company accepted the
scale. "A hearty cheer was given," and contracts, ending June
30, 1894, were immediately drawn up and signed. The Tennessee Company miners had fared well in a situation that
seemed to offer little hope for effective labor pressure. The

Birmingham *Age-Herald,* pleased and satisfied with the outcome of the strike, indulged itself in praise for all concerned. "Here in the Birmingham district," stated the paper, "we have the best class of miners; all in all the most peaceable, law-abiding, and industrious in the country."[73]

While these miners emerged from their struggle with success, others did not fare as well. Late in July the miners of the Sloss Company at Brazil, Blossburg, and Brookside went on strike against wage reductions, and some left the state to seek their fortunes in Pennsylvania and Ohio.[74] In August 1893, the Woodward Mines reduced wages, and trouble developed as some miners went on strike while others continued to work. In October, the *Labor Advocate* charged that the company requested the presence of deputy sheriffs at its mines "as some of the miners are still kicking about a reduction of wages."[75] At the Galloway mines, wages were cut to 40 cents a ton, but no strike resulted. The miners were acutely aware that there were numerous applicants for every job that existed.[76]

In the face of mounting economic pressure, a movement was now generated among the Alabama miners for yet another attempt at a state-wide miners' organization. On October 14, 1893, delegates of the miners met at Bessemer and inaugurated the United Mine Workers of Alabama. Despite the similarity of names, there was to be no national affiliation. Out of their past experiences the Alabama miners were now determined to build a strong union on a state basis and forego the debatable advantages of joining the United Mine Workers of America. Most of the delegates had been instructed to establish an organization with secret membership. This was partially acceded to when open and secret branches were authorized. The union was open to all mine laborers, and local unions were to be established throughout the state. Frank Fournier of Wylam was elected the union's first president, and the Birmingham *Labor Advocate* was selected as the official newspaper of the movement.[77]

Editor Dennis immediately enlisted the *Labor Advocate* in the work of rousing the miners to the need for organization. After reporting that President Fournier was visiting mines unrepresented at the Bessemer meeting, Dennis issued a call for action: "It is there! Rally to the front, Brothers in arms, and let us all do enough work in a month in the way of organizing to last a life-time. . . ."[78] Dennis attempted to explain the nature of the new union to friend and foe. "Let it be understood," he wrote, "that the United Mine Workers of Alabama is not a radical, anarchistic, striking machine, but a body of intelligent workingmen banded together to advance the interest of the calling at which they earn a livelihood."[79] In the heights of his optimism, Dennis advanced the thesis that the union would make strikes unnecessary. The mine owners, he felt, "will watch our every movement, and when they see we mean business, and that everything is going along quietly . . . [with] all disputes and grievances being settled by arbitration, they will dispense with non-union men and employ only those who belong to the Order."[80]

The move to organize came at a crucial time for the Alabama miner, and the response to the new union, if not unanimous, augured well for the future. All through the months of November and December, reports came in of new councils being organized with a swelling membership being enrolled.[81] Significant in the work of organizing was the establishment of several local Negro unions. At most of the mines, two councils were formed, one for whites and the other for Negroes, yet Holman Head reports that a racially mixed council was organized at the mines at Hewitt.[82] It was with clear understanding of the past that Dennis admonished the miners not to "leave our colored Brother out in the cold for a bone of contention. Take him and share and share alike. Educate him on the line. Take care of him and he will do you good."[83]

No union even began its existence under more adverse circumstances than did the United Mine Workers of Alabama. At the time of its organization a strike had been in progress at the mines at Dolomite since the previous August. Caught up in depression difficulties, the mining companies were running behind in their payment of wages, and attempting to solve their problems of overproduction by placing their labor on short work weeks. Even the large Sloss Iron and Steel Company was over a month behind in wage payments. The Tennessee Company mine at Adger had to reduce its work week to two and one-half days.[84]

The Dolomite strike at the Woodward Mines was particularly important because the new union had placed the strike's conduct under its aegis. The strike had been caused by an attempt to lower wages to 34 cents a ton. The strikers complained that the operators had retaliated by importing blacklegs in an effort to continue production.[85] At the end of December, one of the strikers reported that "we are still firm and stand pat, and are determined to stand and battle for the right. . . . Mine operator Woodward is trying to work his mine with incompetent slaves, better known as 'black legs' which he has so far failed to make a success with. . . ." It is evident that there was some truth in the miners' claim that blackleg labor was not efficient. The mine had a normal production of 550 tons per day but during the strike it dropped to 300 tons.[86]

On January 12, 1894, the UMW of Alabama met in convention at Birmingham, and addressed itself to the problem of the Dolomite strike. A committee on the question reported that $1,833 had been collected for strike relief and recommended continuing the strike and providing more financial aid.[87] The union's committee on organization, while reporting general success in organizing, called for co-operation "with the farmer so as to be hand in hand with him always both as producers and consumers."[88]

The Dolomite strike was not resolved until March 20, 1894,

and then it was the solution of defeat. With the acquiescence of the union officers the strike was called off. This first attempt to stop wage reductions under the leadership of the UMW of Alabama ended in failure. Management had been successful in combating the strike with scab labor, and even with financial assistance the Dolomite miners were suffering severe hardship.[89]

The outcome of the Dolomite strike did little to strengthen the UMW, but it did not seriously weaken it. Other difficulties crowded in so quickly that the Dolomite defeat was soon obscured. In January, 1894, reports were heard of rising miner dissatisfaction at the Mary Lee Mines. The miners complained that the company was two months behind in its payment of wages, and while the company was paying $42\frac{1}{2}$ cents per ton, the miners were not allowed to have their own checkweighman to keep the tally on each man's work. When seven miners, angered at not having been paid for two months, left the mine to ask the company for their money, they were summarily fired.[90]

On March 1, far greater troubles descended on the Mary Lee miners. The company announced a wage reduction to 35 cents a ton, with no pay for the "minings"—the dregs that made inferior coke. Since the minings constituted almost a ton of coal a day per miner, the miners contended that the company was really offering wages of about 17 cents per ton. On March 2, a committee called on the operators with a counter offer. They agreed to accept 40 cents a ton "and leave the minings in the mines." This was refused.[91] On March 5, the miners, feeling that wage reductions would not mean more work, voted to go on strike. President Fournier observed that the Mary Lee strike demonstrated that "the cold wave of reduction has reached us, and at an earlier period than a great many of the miners of Alabama expected." The trouble at Mary Lee, said the president, "is but the first shot fired in the state."[92] At the time, the Mary Lee Mines were in receivership. The miners had been unimpressed with the company's claim that it could start up coke ovens and "give regular work" if the miners would accept the 35 cents a ton wage.[93]

It seemed certain that the troubles at Dolomite and Mary Lee were a prelude to general reductions. "Cromwellian," the *Labor Advocate* correspondent from Cardiff, advanced an explanation of the situation. He felt that while the Tennessee Company mines were bound by contract, the smaller companies like Mary Lee, could reduce wages and give the larger companies ample reason to ask for a new contract on the grounds of being competitive. "Cromwellian" warned that "the miners of this State must not allow the reductions to take place one after another at the various mines until there is [sic] only the convict-working companies left unreduced, before they realize this is to become general."[94]

In Walker County, the miners at Corona raised their grievances in demands on the company. There was no question of wage increases, or for that matter even any attempt to maintain the wage level.[95] The Corona men had been reduced to 35 cents a ton without their putting up a struggle, perhaps because as late as January, 1894 they were still working a full week.[96] But they wanted union recognition by the company, and they were particularly insistent that the company reduce its powder prices from $2.25 a keg and lower its house rents. The miners—who at this time used from four to six kegs of powder per month—claimed the company bought its powder at a price of $1.05 and was actually making a profit of at least $6.00 per miner per month.[97] According to the miners, their houses were rented at from $3.00 to $6.00 a month, depending on their size, although none of them was fully sealed against the winter. In such a situation their demands seemed moderate. They agreed to pay $2.00 per keg for powder and asked that rents be set at $1.00 per room per month—a demand which would have reduced a $6.00 house to $4.00.[98]

The manager of Corona left town before the miners' demands

were presented. President Fournier visited the mine in an attempt at peaceful settlement, his actions strongly influenced by
his feeling that the miners had not given the manager an opportunity to consider their proposition. The state president used
his good offices to prevent a strike and a settlement was reached.
The company agreed to reduce the costs of powder to $2.00
per keg, to re-employ some discharged men, and to allow a
bank committee to keep an account of the miners' earnings.[99]

Although little enough had been won in this settlement, the
Birmingham *Labor Advocate* chose to interpret the Corona affair as a victory. "What do you weak and silent members think
of this?" asked the paper. "Is this not proof enough that organization is a power?"[100]

In the month following the settlement at Corona, the miners
there worked only three and three-fourths days. Increased pressure on them now became plainly discernible. At Brookside
the men were working one day a week. At Adger they worked
only eight days during March.[101] No one summed up the
problem more simply than did a miner at Brookside: "We can
hardly live under such conditions and the present prices paid
for digging coal, yet the operators still want to make a reduction."[102] The Tennessee Company miners, working under a
contract wage, were little better off, for their days of work were
reduced. One Tennessee mine was contracted to a private operator who started payment on a per car basis. In this instance
wages were reduced to 32 cents a ton.[103] The operators' position was that their economic situation left them no choice.
They pointed out that a reduction in hours and wages was
preferable to closing down the mines.

As miner income dropped to lower levels it produced two
immediate results: many miners left the state in the hope of
finding work elsewhere, and others, fearful of losing even the
tiny income they had, shunned any identification with the union. [104] There was a close relationship between union affilia-

tion and the political issues of the time. The Birmingham *Labor Advocate* reminded its readers that "there is another battle next Fall that we must all fight. When you go to the polls be sure and cast your ballot for a man who will relieve us from the convict curse."[105] In reporting that the operators at Corona, Coal Valley, and Patton were laying off their miners, "Kentucky," a correspondent for the *Labor Advocate,* pointed out that the firings were coming just as voter registration drew near. The operators, said "Kentucky," wanted to "drive the organized men away thereby disfranchising them, so that the agonized democracy [the organized regular Democrats] can count out beat eighteen as they did last election. But," continued the miner, "we are . . . Kolb men out here and we are going to stay here and keep organization alive and elect our men to office if we have to live in tents to do it."[106]

President Fournier was strongly aware of the dangers that faced his organization. He announced that the mining companies were taking advantage of the depression in what he termed their "piece-meal plan" to reduce the cost of mining. Wages would be reduced at some mines where contracts did not interfere, while at others either little work would be offered or the mine would close completely. Fournier called for a state convention so that the "sense" of each locality could be taken. The depression now gripped the mining industry with its full vigor. The union would have to take action or its membership would wither away. The larger actions of a time of crisis were now at hand.

While no blame could be placed on the coal companies for the existence of the basic cause of trouble—the depression—few of the operators made any effective attempt to lessen the suffering of their miners. The men believed that the operators were attempting to make profits by charging off costs of production—gunpowder, fuses, and tools—to their workers. Rents, the miners complained, were exorbitant, onerous in good times and crushing burdens in a time of depression. In effect, the miners charged that the companies sought to cut losses at the expense of their laborers.

The company store practices and payment in scrip or cash at a discount brought denunciations from the miners. It is probable that the owners paid scrip because the scarcity of working capital left them no choice. The miners, however, interpreted this means of payment as paternalistic and grasping. The Birmingham *Labor Advocate* on June 9, 1894, described the "check system" of payment. According to the paper, the miner was paid by check drawn on the company commissary. If he desired cash, he was forced to take a 25 per cent discount on his check.[107]

Grumbles of complaint had been heard when wages were high and employment strong. Now, as more and more miners seemed headed toward a marginal existence, their complaints grew to protest. No other segment of Alabama labor could better understand the demands of political reformers for improved conditions. Not even the farmer had suffered more from economic distress.

By the spring of 1894, Alabama miners believed themselves victimized and exploited. They were increasingly willing to join the agrarians in giving battle against the status quo and the interests that controlled the state's economic and political structure.

The Strike Begins

On March 30, 1894, the state convention of the United Mine Workers of Alabama met in Birmingham. The officials of the union realized that the time for decision and action had arrived. Mine labor had now been reduced to its lowest level of subsistence, working hours had been reduced and miners had failed to gain desperately needed concessions. Collective action by the miners was now brought into play. It was hoped that operators, faced with organized opposition, would make concessions; but if the reality of miner unity was not enough to gain alleviation, the ultimate weapon of the strike lurked just behind the scenes.

In its first action the state convention appointed a committee to interview the managers of the coal companies. The attitude of the convention was conciliatory, and it ordered its committee to "see if better work could be guaranteed by the miners making proper concessions. . . ."[1] The miners' moderate attitude, it was hoped, might create an atmosphere in which positive steps could be taken for an improvement in management-labor relations.

After conferring only with the operators of the Tennessee Company—the real price and wage setter of the industry—the committee reported its findings to the convention. An agreement on wages between the miners and the Tennessee Company would be tantamount to an agreement with all the operators. The operators stated that while they would not break their present contract, which ran to June 30, 1894, "if the miners would make reasonable concessions, they thought they would be able to go into the market and regain their contracts in iron and coal, put more furnaces in blast and therefore increase the amount of work."[2]

The initial overtures had been made; a spirit of co-operation in the face of common economic problems seemed in evidence. The next step was up to the miners as they defined their version of "reasonable concessions." The convention's committee on scale now went to work, and on Saturday, March 31, the convention approved its deliberations. The miners proposed that a new wage scale should go into operation and that it should govern wages until December 31, 1894. In the new scale, they were willing to take a wage reduction of 10 per cent, providing that the operators would make concessions: all coal would be weighed before it was dumped; the miners would have the right to put a checkweighman on the tipple; and reductions corresponding to the wage cut would be made in house rent, store and mining supplies, and medical costs.[3] From the current 45 cents per ton being paid at the Pratt Mines, the union was offering a reduction to 40½ cents per ton. The qualifications placed on the wage reduction were demands that the miners had made before. They were willing to bargain but any settlement had to be *quid pro quo*.

Having sent its wage offer to the operators, the convention also named a committee to contact the state convict manager and "ascertain what progress if any was being made by the State for the removal of the convicts."[4] With negotiation and inquiry under way, the convention adjourned for the weekend. On Monday, April 2, the committee on convicts reported that the convict manager would have a written statement on the question, but it also addeed that State Senator A. T. Goodwyn, a leading Jeffersonian Democrat, had stated that the convicts would not be out of the mines by January 1, 1895. On the following day the convention voted to have a "monster demonstration" to be called by the president and secretary. Learning that the operators did not plan to answer the wage offer until Wednesday, April 4, the convention adjourned to the following day.[5]

While the state convention waited to hear from the operators, officials of the Tennessee Company had been active at the local level. The operators had never recognized the union as the bargaining agent for their employees, and they now attempted to negotiate directly with their miners on the wage issue. On the night of April 3, officials of the Tennessee Company held a meeting of their miners at Johns, a mine operated exclusively by Negro labor. When the meeting failed to produce any result, the company called another meeting of the Negroes for the following night. Informed of the company's intentions, the white miners of Adger and Sumter attended the second meeting on the night of April 4. The uninvited guests were coldly received by the company officials, but the Negro miners, in more cordial mood, voted to make the affair a joint meeting. The company spokesmen then made the same wage offer that had been made that day to the miners' convention in Birmingham.[6]

The counter offer of the operators showed a great disparity of interpretation on the substance of "reasonable concessions." Where the miners had offered to accept a wage reduction of 10 per cent, the operators suggested a reduction of 22½ per cent.

The company agreed to reduce house rent by only 10 per cent and to make some indefinite reductions in the cost of power and supplies.[7] The miners interpreted the Tennessee Company's action as an attempt to by-pass the deliberations of the state convention. As one miner suggested, its "intention was to cajole and coax Johns to take the reduction, Adger and Sumteer was [sic] to follow, then Pratt and Blocton, and of course the rest of the State would fall into line."[8]

On Thursday, April 5, the Tennessee miners' delegates to the state convention reported to their constituents at a mass meeting held at Johns. The assembled miners unanimously instructed their delegates to reject the company's offer when they returned to the convention.

Despite the opposition to the company offer, the Tennessee Company made yet another attempt to bargain directly with its employees. On Friday morning, April 6, officials of the company called a meeting of the miners inside one of the mines, probably either Adger or Sumter. The meeting was short and to the point. The operators stated that they hoped the miners would take the reduction. The miners replied that they could not take formal action on the question until they heard from their state convention. The officials then left the mine, and according to union men, locked the recalcitrant miners inside. When the miners discovered their plight they managed to break down the doors with axes. A protest meeting was held in the afternoon, and the actions of the company officials were denounced.[9]

An auspicious beginning in wage negotiations thus ended in petty and dangerous disagreement. The Tennessee Company made it clear that it was opposed to dealing with the union as the miners' spokesman. The miners believed that the operators were determined to sacrifice the well-being of their employees in an effort to serve the demands of profit and property. In this atmosphere there was little hope of amicable compromise. The miners' state convention rejected the offer of the Tennessee Company and asked that "the old scale be paid in all mines in the State. . . ."[10] When this was refused, the state convention voted for a strike by all of its members to begin on April 14, 1894.[11]

Although the Alabama miners had acted entirely on their own, the depressed conditions that had led them to their strike decision were universal throughout the coal mining industry. On April 10, 1894, the United Mine Workers of America held its fifth annual meeting in Columbus, Ohio. John McBride, president of the UMW, proposed a general strike. As McBride put it, "the price paid for mining must go no lower, but it is absolutely necessary for both life and comfort, and you are entitled to both, that the price should go higher, and that soon."[12] In support of its president, the convention called for a strike to begin on Saturday, April 21, in an effort to restore wages to their level at the beginning of the year.[13]

While the Alabama miners received national reinforcement in their strike effort, it was the reinforcement of common endeavor rather than that of material strike relief. The United Mine Workers of Alabama had called the strike without reference to national union plans, and they were to make their fight in the same isolated fashion.

As the Alabama miners prepared to implement their strike on April 14, both sides of the controversy addressed themselves to the public in rationalization and justification of their positions. The executive committee of the Alabama miners explained:

The 22½ per cent reduction proposed by the T.C.I.R.R. Co., the extensive operation of their commisary and check system, and the employment of from two to three times as many miners as actually needed, to make the commissary profitable and keep the

labor in a dependent and unsettled condition, means a virtual
enslavement of the miners and the turning of our nineteenth
century civilization back into its barbaric past. . . .[14]

On the very eve of the strike, the Tennessee Company's Vice-
President DeBardeleben assumed direction of affairs for the
operators. Hard working, able, and given to the use of the flam-
boyant phrase, DeBardeleben in personality and position was
a first class antagonist. It is important to point out that his
actions throughout the strike were based on promoting the
company, and there is no evidence to indicate that he was hostile to the laboring class. For that matter, the Tennessee Company faced the hard fact of economic survival and did not fit
the stereotype of the "soulless corporation."

On April 13, DeBardeleben stated the operators' position in a
letter to the Birmingham *Age-Herald*. It was plain that he regarded the miners' strike as a declaration of war, a war that
he had no intention of losing.[15] He defended the company's
policy of subcontracting its separate mines, and added that if
the so-called "Division" system of dividing the miners made
them easier to handle "there is nothing left for us to do but to
contract to such parties as can cope with and handle labor.
. . ."[16] On this point the *Labor Advocate* replied that DeBardeleben could divide his miners as much as he liked, but he
would still find "a solid array of organized labor with one
proposition."[17]

Specifically attacking the miners' position on the wage question, DeBardeleben pointed out that "all classes of labor that
are connected with the manufacture of pig iron . . . have
come down except the price of mining coal, which remains
where it was when the iron was selling for double the present
price."[18] He thought the miners partly responsible for low
productivity but failed to mention that the company could
not sell the pig iron already produced. He continued that to
have only four furnaces running "is something that is very

distasteful and too cowardly for my nature . . . to tamely submit to for fear of offending the boys that are working under ground."[19] The company resolved to bring the cost of mining into line "if it takes four years of the war."[20]

Reacting to the developing strike, the state press began to interpret events for its readers. The moderate Bessemer *Weekly* observed that the company's wage offer, even with full-time work, would make a great difference in miner earnings, "and have rather of a disastrous effect upon trade generally." The paper spoke for compromise, while observing that "the sharp, unmistakable tendency is lower wages and even at lower wages a less demand for labor."[21] The Birmingham *Age-Herald,* sympathetic to the coal and iron companies, argued that the strike would not affect the iron industry since convict-mined coal could meet the local demand. Never, said the paper, had a strike "come at so unfortunate a time and at so critical a juncture." Past experience showed that the miners could not win their strike, and in such depressed times they would be better advised to worry about their jobs rather than about their pay.[22] Just one day earlier, the Bessemer *Weekly* had reported that "fortunately for the Tennessee Company they have sufficient convict labor to mine ample coal to keep their four furnaces now in blast going, and to furnish the other industries here with fuel."[23] The miners could not stop convict production without resort to outright violence and illegality.

While the Bessemer *Weekly* was saddened by the strike, and the *Age-Herald* sought to minimize its effect, the pro-labor Bessemer *Journal* forthrightly defended the miners:

That the miners have been working for almost starvation wages for some time, is a fact that no one will deny, and it was but the instincts of self-preservation that made them resist any further reduction in their wages. The company, however, claimed that it was absolutely necessary to make these reductions, but it does seem that they should have been satisfied when the miners voluntarily came forward and offered to accept a 10 per cent reduction which reduced their wages on an average to about $20.00 per month. But the company was not satisfied and demanded a cut that would leave the miners about $16.00 a month. . . . Can anyone blame the miners for not accepting it?[24]

During the strike's first three weeks there were two basic developments of consequence. The first of these centered on the attempt by the union to involve all miners in the strike effort; the second concerned the strategy of the operators in their effort to put down the labor uprising.

On April 14, approximately 6,000 miners heeded the call of their union and joined the strike. Since the initial difficulties had concerned the Tennessee Company and its employees, the miners at the other mines had to be enlisted in joint effort. Of particular importance were the mines in Walker County, for their production was second only to Jefferson.

A mass meeting of miners was held at Oakman in Walker County on April 21, with representation from the major mines at Corona, Patton, Black Diamond, Lockhart, Coal Valley, and Gas Light. The miners reported that they were all out on strike except "a few men" still at work at Patton who were expected to join the strike in a few days.[25] All the miners at Corona had joined the strike, although their wages had not been reduced.[26] The meeting adopted resolutions calling for a pay scale of 55 cents a ton, and demanded of the companies "that no man be victimized or no work to resume under any circumstances."[27]

The importance of the Walker County mass meeting was denied by the F. C. Dunn Company, the operator of the mines at Patton and Coal Valley. The company announced that work would go on "as usual," and that a strong guard of deputy sheriffs would be present at both mines to protect nonstriking miners.[28] With rumors abroad that the strikers would use force to keep the miners at Patton from going to work, the Birmingham *Age-Herald* sent a reporter to Patton to record the may-

hem. In the first of many anticlimaxes, the miners at Patton
went peacefully to their work, guarded, as the reporter stated,
"by a force of deputies under a gamey sheriff."[29] (The sheriff
of Walker County at this time was G. H. Guttery.) The miners
at Patton were the exception to the rule. During the strike's first
week the union gained adherents to its cause, and the Birmingham *Age-Herald* stated that 9,000 miners were out on strike.
This was an exaggerated estimate of very real union gains.[30]
The miners at Little Warrior "signed a paper" to stop
work until the issue was settled, and when five men refused to
sign, the strikers had their names published in the Birmingham
Labor Advocate, April 12, 1894.

At the Tennessee Company's mines, the hard core of the
strike, the work stoppage began with good humor but dire
portent. According to "Pendragon," writing from Blue Creek
for the *Labor Advocate,* company officials were particularly
angered when no Negro miners appeared for work on Monday,
April 16, at their mine at Johns. "Pendragon" wrote that the
company had "always had the idea that because there was
[sic] only colored men employed at Johns . . . they could do
anything they like with them. They have found out their mis-
take and it has dawned upon their somewhat clouded vision
that the colored men down here are just as wide awake to their
own interests as the white men are."[31]

During the strike's first weekend, before it became clear that
the miners would not appear for work, a railroad car loaded
with company officials was dispatched to Johns. A party was
held in the car on Saturday night (the day the strike went into
effect), and it was rumored that alcoholic drinks were liberally
dispensed. Reporting on the affair, "Pendragon" sarcastically
observed:

> I never realized how kind and indulgent the Tennessee . . . Com-
> pany really were until a few days past. How very thoughtful and
> interested they were about their employees welfare. Here they

are coming down here to help us pass the long dreary hours away
by filling us full of beer and whiskey and lulling us to sleep with
dulcet strains of a string band composed of one negro and a
banjo.[32]

When the miners failed to reconsider their position, the company took additional measures on May 16. All of its miners at
Johns, Adger, and Sumter were ordered to vacate their houses
and company premises. None of the miners heeded this injunc-
tion since they had not been paid. "Pendragon" reported that
it was "only another bluff and like all the others it didn't
work."[33]

The Tennessee Company, however, was no less determined
than the miners. DeBardeleben, as the *Age-Herald* put it, "has
had confided to him the management of this struggle," and he
was quick to lay his plans for counteraction.[34] Without dealing
with the methods to be employed, DeBardeleben announced on
April 18 that "the struggle will soon be over; Johns will be at
work tomorrow. I will entertain Fort Sumter as soon as I can
pump the water out. Fort Adger will be besieged after the capture of Fort Sumter."[35]

There was substance behind DeBardeleben's hyperbole. His
strategy in breaking the strike was to import Negro labor to
work the mines. During the strike's first week 100 Negroes were
brought in from Kansas. Newspapers reported that L. W. Johns,
general superintendent of the Tennessee Company, was making arrangements to import an additional 200 Negroes for the
Blue Creek mines.[36] The use of Negroes as strikebreakers was
a calculated risk that seemed likely to add racial antipathy to
the strikers' strong aversion to blackleg labor. If enough Negroes could be sent into the mines the strike would be broken.
Although no violence had yet occurred, the employment of
strikebreakers made disorder more probable. Since the strikers
would object strongly to scab labor, its employment would be
possible only with the protection of county and state law en-

forcement. The strikers complained that from the first there was never a question as to the attitude of law enforcement officials. Company guards, the strikers charged, were regularly deputized in whatever numbers the companes desired. According to the Mobile *Daily News,* the operators met on the night of May 6 and it was reported that "complete protection both by state and counties is assured and systematically arranged."[37]

The union was alive to the dangers posed by the use of blackleg labor. The *Labor Advocate* asked: "What will be the effect of importing degraded and deluded negro laborers to take their [the strikers'] places? The severing of the bonds of their family altars and turning them out upon the world to subsist by charity or commit crime to sustain life."[38]

The union's executive committee issued an announcement for a "monster demonstration" to be held in Lake View Park in Birmingham on April 23. Speeches were promised by Jeffersonian State Senator A. T. Goodwyn, by two men who were the miners' candidates for the state legislature, and by "other well known local talent of the various mines."[39]

Coincident with the call for a public demonstration of the miners' cause, rumors of violence began to be heard for the first time. On April 22 the *Age-Herald* reported that DeBardeleben, "who has been instrumental in placing negro labor" in the mines, had received an anonymous letter "at the bottom of which was drawn a coffin and cross bones. The letter was threatening and talked of blood if existing wishes of the striking miners were not acceded to." The paper also published reports "that the miners have organized volunteer companies, and that drilling for intended action is going on. Exactly to what extent this is being done is not known." The conservative Mobile *Daily News* printed the same type of unverified information,[40] reporting that on the night of April 22, the houses of blacklegs at Johns were fired into. Both newspapers indicated the unverified nature of their reports, but an image of violence was created in the public mind long before violence in fact occurred.

Among those worried that the miners' demonstration might result in open violence against company property, or in an attempt to free the convicts at the mines was Governor Jones. On April 22, Jones received a telegram from Sheriff George M. Morrow of Jefferson County: "Trouble anticipated tomorrow; situation grave; troops may be needed. Would suggest that Gatling guns be sent at once to Col. Clark."[41] Col. L. V. Clark was commanding officer of the second regiment of the Alabama state troops. Reacting to this warning of trouble, Governor Jones journeyed to Birmingham on Sunday, April 22, discussed the situation with Sheriff Morrow and made arrangements for the local Birmingham militia to report to their armory at two hour intervals throughout the following day.[42]

The next morning, before the demonstration had started, Governor Jones held a two hour conference with the executive committee of the miners' union in order to "place responsibility" on the miners for the maintenance of order.[43] He informed the committee members that he had heard of miners drilling for action, and he particularly took issue with banners that had been prepared for the demonstration. These streamers bore such slogans as "Out With The Convicts" and "The Convicts Must Go." The executive members replied that they wanted the convicts removed but that they intended to accomplish their purpose lawfully. Jones then informed the members that the state authorities were not charged with any functions concerning the strike, and that as long as peace was maintained they would do nothing to affect it. The meeting closed as the governor told the committee members that prevention of violence rested with them. "The committee promised to do all in its power; but admitted there were a number of miners whom it could not control and for whom it would not answer."[44]

With the eyes of the governor upon them, some 4,000 miners gathered for their demonstration, at least one-half of them Negroes.[45] They marched to Lake View Park carrying their banners emblazoned with slogans of "Give Us Our Daily Bread," "United We Stand," "Convicts Must Go," "No De-Bardeleben Beer Wanted By The Miners," and "We, The Colored Miners of Alabama, Stand With Our White Brothers."[46] Once at the park, the demonstrators were quiet and orderly, despite the report of the Mobile *Daily News* that it looked "ominous."[47]

President Fournier informed the assembled miners of the conference held with Governor Jones, warning them that ". . . the law is against us if we do not behave ourselves as law-abiding citizens."[48] Further speechmaking followed, the tenor well illustrated by the remarks of S. F. Marion, a miner from Cardiff, who blamed Wall Street for the economic depression and attacked DeBardeleben for his importation of strikebreaking labor.[49] The meeting adjourned after adopting resolutions reiterating past demands and vowing to continue the strike.

Governor Jones had put credence in rumors of miner violence, but in his meeting with the executive committee he had shown no particular animosity to the miners' cause. Jones remained in Birmingham for several days following the Lake View demonstration, and on April 27, he held another meeting with union officials where the question of violence was again the topic of conversation. At the conclusion of the meeting, the governor made a public statement. He believed that "many of the dispatches being sent from this district were viciously sensational and give rise to the most unfounded and unjust opinions of the attitude of the bulk of the miners."[50]

The governor acted properly in attempting to play down the journalistic sensationalism of the time, although his statement was not an indication that his own fears had been allayed. His interpretation of the opening rounds of the strike was that while conservative miners checked "open acts of violence," the strike was ushered in:

> with intimidation and threats against the persons and property of those who continued to work. Apprehension that these threats would be carried out, caused many appeals to the civil authorities for protection, resulting in the stationing of scores of deputies around the mines, which further intensified feeling.[51]

His analysis, in the opinion of the strikers, did not accurately consider the question of cause and effect. Miner threats were not the genesis of the companies' demand for protection by deputies. The miners claimed that the operators asked for protection after their importation of blackleg labor. Once the importation had begun, miner hatred for these men made the presence of the deputies more plausible.

As the strike continued into its third week, the outlines of the conflict were plainly delineated. At least 8,000 miners were on strike, and DeBardeleben's earlier pronouncements on a "speedy resumption of work" were now seen to have been "rather premature."[52] An "unexpected" feature of the strike was the "stubborness [sic] and unity" of the Negro miners, who seemed "as determined in their purpose as the white."[53] One Negro miner reported that he could have made $50 a month at scab wages, but "I struck because the others did and white miners were very urgent that we should stand with them."[54] Newspapers took outspoken positions. When the Birmingham *Age-Herald* announced that "the backbone of the strike is broken," the Bessemer *Journal* retorted that this was a "puerile attempt of a certain corporation sheet to dishearten the miners . . . in keeping with the many queer emanations from that source."[55] For good measure the *Journal* made plain its opposition to the Tennessee Company.[56]

The miners' executive committee reported that the strike

was proceeding smoothly and that all indications pointed to victory. Such optimistic statements were qualified by reports that miners were already being jailed on charges of intimidation of blacklegs. It was claimed that one member of the executive committee was arrested for trespassing when he called at the postoffice for his mail. The postoffice was located in the company's offices.[57] The executive committee called on all trade unions and the Farmers' Alliance for financial aid in carrying on the strike.[58]

During the strike's third week, the Bessemer *Weekly* sent a reporter on a tour of the Tennessee Company's mines. According to the reporter, the strike now centered on the "determination of Mr. DeBardeleben to Africanize the labor."[59] While the importation of non-union labor had not proceeded as swiftly as DeBardeleben had hoped, more Negroes were coming in, and by May 2, production at Johns and Sumter had reached 759 tons a day.[60] At the mines at Adger the reporter found all the miners out on strike. Although ordered to vacate the company's property, few of the miners had left. The strikers scoffed at the company's claim that full-time work would follow a reduction in wages. "Were they to accept the reduction they would soon be again at the mercy of short time and irregular demand."[61] Although cash was already running low, the miners were in good spirits, and supplies of bread and meat, contributed by Birmingham labor unions, were arriving at the miners' commissary.

While touring the mines at Sumter, the reporter encountered DeBardeleben who was in "his usual good spirits."[62] DeBardeleben stated that things were going well. He claimed that several white miners had asked to get their jobs back but he refused

as he had formed the resolution not to use white miners in any of the Blue Creek mines. He said he had had so much trouble with them, their striking so often without cause and their persistent dissatisfaction that he had come to the conclusion that it was to the interest of the company to confine mining in the Blue Creek section to the colored race, that none of the white miners had vested interests there. . . . He said the resolution was unalterable, and hence he would require every white miner to vacate the company's premises.[63]

In the mind of the roving reporter, DeBardeleben's determination settled the issue of the strike once and for all. He heard no threats or talk of violence on the part of the strikers. The presence of a Captain Sharp and a squad of deputy sheriffs seemed to re-inforce DeBardeleben's final victory. In a spirit of acquiescence to the inevitable, the reporter concluded that "it seems rather sad and a mockery of fate that white people should be made to give way to the colored race. . . ."[64]

One fact was clear beyond equivocation. Unless the miners could halt the use of blacklegs their cause was lost. Peaceful persuasion of the strikebreakers to stop work was useless, and the thin line between persuasion and intimidation would have been breached in any event. Violence was endemic in the situation.

chapter 4

Violence and State Troops

With the coal mine strike only three weeks old, the miners seemed in serious danger of losing not only the strike but any chance of regaining their old jobs. Slowly but surely the operators were obtaining the blackleg labor necessary to carry on and increase production. If the operators' strategy continued unchecked, the strike promised to end in the devastating defeat both of the union and its members. Many of the striking miners, realizing the threat that hung over them, knew as well that dealing with the blackleg problem did not constitute a choice of alternatives between legal and illegal methods. Only through intimidation could the blacklegs be driven out of the mines, and any effective action on the part of the strikers was dangerous to themselves and to their cause. Did the risks of using intimidation outweigh the risks of avoiding it? To some miners there seemed to be a chance of victory if intimidation were used; there was certain defeat if the strikers remained quiescent.

If an attempt were made to frighten scab labor from the mines it would have to be done by individual groups of miners, acting on their own volition and initiative. The union's executive committee, aware of the realities of state power and desiring a favorable public opinion for the miners' cause, roundly condemned violence on the part of its members. What now occurred among the strikers was leadership from the ranks.

On the night of May 6, about fifty men, "assumed to be strikers," marched on Price's Mines at Horse Creek. The miners at Price's had refused to join the strike and had continued to work. Retaliation now fell upon them. The boilers, machinery, and headings of the mine were dynamited, and the mine was effectively put out of production.[1] Following the attack on Price's, an unsuccessful attempt was made to set fire to the tipple at the nearby Victor Mines.[2] With its mission at least partially accomplished, the raiding party, as Governor Jones later reported, "dispersed so quickly that pursuit was not practicable."[3]

Reaction to the Horse Creek affair was immediate. The Bessemer *Journal,* a strong supporter of the miners' cause, regretted that "a few hot-headed miners . . . have seriously jeopardized the success of the strike by committing deeds of violence and destroying property."[4] The *Labor Advocate* attempted a brave front, maintaining that the whole affair was "almost wholly without foundation and viciously circulated to injure the miners' cause."[5] After implying that little if anything had occurred at Horse Creek, the paper then suggested that the company itself had caused the damage "as a big sympathy racket."[6] As if realizing that this charge made little sense, the editor got down to reality with the observation that "the public should remember that there are something like 7,000 heads of families in our midst virtually facing starvation. . . ."[7]

Governor Jones, who had feared "serious commotions and turbulence" since the beginning of the strike, was moved to greater action.[8] The governor offered a $400 reward for the

conviction of the guilty parties in the Horse Creek affair, and
on the morning of May 7, he wired the miners' executive committee asking for its co-operation in locating the participants.[9]
Two days later he met with the committee and secured their
promise "to ascertain the truth as to who were guilty of the outrages at Horse Creek."[10] Subsequently, the executive committee, accompanied by Lt. James B. Erwin, a United States Army
officer on duty with the Alabama troops, visited Horse Creek
and submitted a report to the governor. According to Erwin,
the investigation "clearly proves that this act was done by striking miners."[11] Ten days after the meeting with Governor
Jones, the executive committee issued a public statement in
order to "openly denounce any act of violence that has been
committed by any party or parties." The committee stated its
desire "to win a bloodless victory, and any acts of intimidation
or violence will necessarily be detrimental to our cause. . . ."[12]

Having publicly reinforced the efforts to apprehend the
Horse Creek rioters, Governor Jones took other action. Immediately after the affair, he had dispatched Lt. Erwin to Birmingham, where his arrival was reported by the press. It was
explained that he represented Governor Jones and was "investigating the condition of affairs."[13] Unknown to the public,
the press, and certainly to the miners was the role that Lt. Erwin
would play in what the governor later referred to as "arrangements for promptly gathering and receiving intelligence of any
change in the situation."[14] Erwin's job was to co-ordinate the
activities of a private investigator and a group of Pinkerton
detectives that Governor Jones had retained. The employment
of detectives in labor disorders was opposed by the strikers but
was common practice throughout the country.

The first of the detectives to join Lt. Erwin in Birmingham
was T. N. Vallens, who was already operating in the state. Vallens had been employed as a political investigator by Governor
Jones as early as September 1891. When the coal mine strike

began he had been investigating the activities of militant agrarian "White Cappers" in South Alabama.[15] Besides Lt. Erwin and Vallens, Governor Jones had three Pinkerton detectives sent to Birmingham during May, although he later observed that he had asked for only two and the third was sent without consulting him. One of the Pinkerton men was J. H. Foley, described by Lt. Erwin as "the man for the place in education, manners, speech, dress, and is a miner. Yesterday he reports as getting in with the very crowd we have not before been able to reach."[16] The other two detectives were shadowy figures identified only as "E. W." and "J. M. P."

As the governor's agents prepared to swing into action, more violence followed the Horse Creek dynamiting. On the night of May 10, a reputed 700 miners held a meeting in the woods near the Pratt Mines. The meeting ended without trouble, but later in the night some forty miners "began to bother some coal" near one of the mines and were fired on by two of the company guards. The miners returned the fire, "and for a few minutes a regular fusillade took place." After both sides encountered the difficulties of night firing, the miners left the scene of action.[17] In further exacerbation of the feelings of both sides, four miners were arrested on May 10, for participating in the Horse Creek affair. A fifth man was supposedly arrested and then "rescued" by a band of fifteen miners.[18]

The atmosphere was one of mounting tension and gave every evidence of increasing violence. Governor Jones and Lt. Erwin met on May 13 to concert their plan of action. The plan agreed upon was an attempt to guarantee the observance of law and order. It was decided, in Lt. Erwin's words, "to get the operators to open up again, assuring them and their miners of protection. . . ."[19] As interpreted by the strikers, this plan greatly reduced their chances of success. The power of the state, it seemed to them, now lay behind the resumption of operations using strikebreakers. The strikers contended that in the name of preventing violence the operators were being urged to speed up the very process that engendered it.

Since the strike's beginning, the miners' executive committee had been occupied in attempts to stiffen the strike effort while avoiding violence. President Fournier, busy directing the strike, nevertheless found time to organize four new union councils at Blocton, Warrior, Carbon Hill, and Gurnee.[20] On May 9, members of the executive committee saw newspaper reports that an interstate conference between operators and the United Mine Workers of America was scheduled for Cleveland, Ohio, on May 15. Eager to find a method by which to end their strike, the executive committee wired President John McBride of the national union to ask if he would accord representation to the Alabama miners. When McBride replied affirmatively, the executive committee issued an invitation to the Alabama operators "to meet with us . . . and . . . come to an agreement of a national character that will be lasting. . . ."[21]

With an eye on national developments, Editor Dennis of the *Labor Advocate* supported the Cleveland conference. Dennis felt that the "operators should come together and say what they will sell their coal and iron for and agree with labor as to what it will pay. Nothing less will settle the trouble. . . ." Labor unrest marked the beginning of "radical changes in the government." If these changes did not come peacefully, they would come "by revolution if necessary."[22]

President Fournier represented his union at the Cleveland conference, but he found that only four operators from all of Tennessee and Alabama were present. Neither nationally nor on an Alabama level did the conference accomplish its purpose. The operators were almost unanimously in favor of wage reductions; the miners favored retention of the old scale. The Alabama operators did not feel it imperative to settle the strike. While they had no coal reserves on hand, convict and non-union labor production was meeting their needs.[23]

Lt. Erwin, still in Birmingham, asked the governor to keep him informed of proceedings at the conference. He knew that the strikers were interested in the outcome, "and perhaps much here will depend upon the action of the conference; though we are rendering them [the strikers] less and less powerless [sic] every day."[24]

When at length the Cleveland conference ended in failure, the Alabama strike reverted to its own course. Except for minor victories the tide now seemed to go strongly against the union. DeBardeleben continued his efforts to hire blackleg labor, and by May 26 it was reported that he had raised production at the Blue Creek mines to its normal 1,800 tons a day.[25] His actions, not unexpectedly, earned him criticism in several quarters,[26] and one miner pointed out that the Bourbons sought economic aid from Negroes but preached white supremacy in politics.[27] On May 21, DeBardeleben brought an additional twenty Negroes to the Blue Creek mines; Aldrich had imported thirty blacklegs the previous week.[28] The Tennessee Company concentrated its efforts at Pratt and Blue Creek, and made no effort to reopen its Blocton mines. When a fire broke out in one of the abandoned mines at Blocton, the *Labor Advocate* sarcastically announced that "Gov. Jones should at once hurry up with another proclamation of $400 for the dastardly perpetrators."[29]

The other operators, at the urging of Governor Jones, also began to resume operations. Thomas O. Seddon of the Sloss Company placed blackleg labor in his mines at Blossburg, Brookside, and Coalburg,[30] and Lt. Erwin, observing the Sloss operation, noted that it had not led to any "action on the part of the strikers." Erwin felt that the process was "beneficial in the extreme" since "conservative" miners would now see that their strike was ineffectual.[31] At Brookside sixty blacklegs were at work, guarded by fifty deputies. With the deputies being paid $2.50 a day, one miner observed that "we can't see where the profits will be as there was about one guard per man."[32] The

Labor Advocate inelegantly reported that Patton, like the other mines, had a "big force of black-leg coons."[33]

While the strikers maintained a spirit of defiance, their position grew steadily worse. Deputies arrested miners who threatened or molested blacklegs in the exercise of their right "to work or not to work."[34] Eleven men supposedly connected with the Horse Creek dynamiting were arrested.[35] Intimidation won a small victory for the strikers when Negro blacklegs at the mine at Milldale refused to work. The Negroes had been warned to quit work by notices decorated with daggers, pistols, and cross bones, and signed with blood.[36]

Coincident with the growing use of non-union labor, the operators attempted to evict all strikers from company houses and property. The action provoked vastly different interpretations. The miners brought charges of inhumanity, although the operators had a point in questioning the logic of providing housing for workers pledged to injure the company. Mass ejectment suits were filed at Coalburg, Brookside, and Blossburg. As one observer noted, being forced to leave their houses when the company still owed them wages created "a fever heat of indignation" among the strikers.[37] At Hewitt, strikers met to elect a relief committee "to beg for us," but a company official countered with an offer to any striker of wages of 67 cents a ton if he would return to work. The *Labor Advocate* claimed that when the strikers refused to negotiate except through their union they were served with notices of eviction.[38] When the striking miners were evicted from their homes at Adger they built log huts for themselves on private property owned by a sympathetic farmer.[39] Evicted from their homes and having gone in many cases for two months without pay, the strikers existed on contributions. Supplies of flour, meat, and corn came in to stock little commissaries they established. The executive committee distributed supplies purchased with the monetary contributions that came in large numbers and small amounts,[40] while the *Labor Advocate* regularly published lists of contributors to strike relief.

Lt. Erwin, surveying the situation, felt that it was simply a matter of time before the strike would be broken. He reported that it was in effect over, although "it will be all of a month before they [the strikers] submit to the inevitable, and leave here, as the operators will not again employ them."[41] This optimism, however, was not shared by Detective Vallens. Vallens admitted that the miners "are very destitute," but he added that "at present they know the company [the Tennessee Company] is operating at a heavy loss, and if the miners can keep the company from adding to their present force they think they will win."[42]

Up to this point, violence and intimidation on the part of the strikers had paid few dividends. The very impotence of their economic power, and the realization that they had already lost homes and jobs, kindled their anger and incited some of them to strike back at the operators and the hated blacklegs. On May 16, Chat Holman, a Negro who had not joined the strike, was fired upon during the morning. Later in the day when he went into Pratt City he was arrested on a warrant sworn out by the strikers, charging him with carrying concealed weapons. When Holman was jailed, a crowd gathered and in surly mood began to talk of lynching him. T. H. Aldrich, hearing of the situation, came to the jail, bailed Holman out, and took him to the safety of the company's furnaces as the crowd belabored the two men with rocks and mud.[43]

On the Sunday morning of May 20, the first bloodshed of the strike occurred. Walter Glover, a Negro blackleg who was recruiting other Negroes for the company, was killed by a shot fired through the front door of his house. Sheriff Morrow arrived from Birmingham and arrested Con Sullivan and Jere Hilliary, white miners, and John Driver, a Negro, for the murder. Morrow claimed that the circumstantial evidence against Sullivan and Driver was strong. Driver had a bullet wound in his side, supposedly caused by the shots of pursuing deputies. The evidence against Sullivan consisted of a hole in his hat. Sheriff Morrow insisted that it was a bullet hole, while Sullivan maintained that rats had eaten it.[44] On Sunday afternoon the miners held a protest meeting at Pratt and denied Morrow's right to arrest the men. The strikers insisted that no miners were involved in the shooting, and that the murder was the result of firing by the guards "simply to bring on a fight that they might hold their jobs."[45] On May 24, Sullivan and Driver were indicted for murder by a Birmingham jury.[46]

Governor Jones later claimed that a group of striking miners assembled "for the purpose of releasing the convicts by force, and abandoned their contemplated attack solely because their leader, failing in courage, surrendered to the sheriff. . . ."[47] No corroborative evidence of the governor's story has been found, but there were many rumors that the strikers planned to free the convicts.[48]

Following the murder of Glover, events moved rapidly toward a culmination. On May 21, Vallens assured the governor that there was no danger of an attack on the convicts, but that it was now questionable whether the operators could get "any considerable number" of Negroes to go to work "as they are much frightened."[49] This threatened the state's pledge to maintain law and order. If the strike was to be broken with blackleg labor, the state now had to provide effective protection.

Lt. Erwin's report to Governor Jones on May 22 contained opositive recommendations for action. Although Erwin still felt that the strike was broken, he feared a final act of desperation by the strikers. A general feeling of security would follow the speedy trial and punishment of "Sullivan and others" for the murder of Glover, but something more was needed to prevent future attacks.[49] Although Erwin knew the governor's "hesitancy to order troops here," he had "thought of this matter very seriously," and therefore recommended that "the regular encampment of all State Troops" be held at Ensley.[51] He believed that "trained soldiers, wearing the uniform of the State, and ordered here not to suppress the strikers, but for the usual encampment, will have a most decidedly quieting effect. . . ."[52]

Lt. Erwin informed the governor that he had already investigated accommodations for the troops. Water, lights, and buildings would be given "without one cent of cost, and $4,000 will be raised here if you will order the regiments . . . into camp at Ensley."[53] The Tennessee Company had promised to aid in providing necessary facilities,[54] and since the assistant general manager of the company, G. B. McCormack, had written Erwin to confirm the offer of financial assistance,[55] it seems probable that Erwin had discussed the question of bringing in the state troops with the officials of the Tennessee Company before he recommended it to the governor. The origin of the suggestion for troop use is unknown, but in his public report Lt. Erwin implied that it was first suggested by Sheriff Morrow, who felt that "sooner or later . . . it would be necessary to call upon the military of the state."[56] Certainly the strikers would object to the presence of the militia, and the operators would regard the move favorably.

From Governor Jones's viewpoint, the plan suggested by Erwin had particular merit. It would be better to send the state troops into regular training encampment where they could be called on if needed in the strike, than simply to order the troops into the coal fields. On the other hand, the troops could not be used to put down violence unless a sheriff certified his inability to maintain law and order and asked the governor to intervene.

On May 24, Erwin telegraphed Jones and informed him that Sheriff Morrow had written asking that troops be called out,[57] and one day later the governor received Sheriff Morrow's assertion that he was unable to keep the peace with the forces at his disposal. The sheriff cited the murder of Glover, the riotous events following the arrest of Holman, and the existence of armed groups "roaming in parts of the county" as the basis of his call for reinforcements.[58] On the same day Governor Jones replied to the sheriff promising that troops would be sent. As the governor phrased it, "the honor of the state, the saving of bloodshed and the supremacy of law all require the action you suggest and your views are heartily approved."[59]

Governor Jones's alarm was sincere, and he took pains to explain to the press that it was time for an annual encampment in any event, although he added that the main reason for the muster was to control lawlessness during the coal strike.[60] Lt. Erwin announced that the encampment would be "an era in Alabama's military history" and that the strictest discipline would be enforced.[61]

The Birmingham *Age-Herald* applauded the governor's action in calling out the troops while claiming that up to this point it had "patiently avoided criticisms of the action of the striking miners. . . ."[62] The newspaper was convinced that "bloodshed seems to be inevitable, as the situation grows more threatening."[63] The Black Belt Union Springs *Herald* felt that "Governor Jones again deserves the praise of his state for the manner in which he has conducted things in so trying a time."[64] The Tuscaloosa *Gazette* admired the "governor's grit in this matter. . . "[65] Opposition to the governor's move was slower in developing, but it would be heard from in full measure as the strike continued.

chapter **5**

Violence and a Quieter Note

As the second regiment of the Alabama state troops began to assemble for its muster at the newly christened Camp Forney at Ensley, plans were laid by the striking miners to show their disapproval of the governor's intervention. On May 25, when it was learned that Sheriff Morrow had requested troops and that Governor Jones had agreed to send them, a mass meeting was called for the following day in Birmingham. Detective Vallens, reporting the news of the proposed gathering to the governor, felt that the meeting was "called at the instigation of some politicians who desire to show their sympathy for the miners in order to catch their vote—it will have no good effect on the situation. . . ."[1]

On May 26, almost 1,000 miners assembled at Pratt City in mass meeting. Although they discussed the questions raised by the intervention of the state troops, they contented themselves with passing a resolution criticizing Sheriff Morrow in calling for troops and did not mention Governor Jones's role in supplying them.[2] With some disposition made of the subject of military intervention, the strikers turned their attention to policies of their own. A committee was appointed to meet with the operators to explore the possibilities of a strike settlement, and another committee was established to call on all the railroad unions and request them to adopt policies against hauling any coal mined by blackleg labor. This latter move constituted a new direction in miner strategy. Having failed to halt coal production, the men realized that pressure could be placed on the operators just as effectively if the transportation of coal could be stopped.[3]

With their business concluded, the strikers marched into Birmingham in mass demonstration. Even Detective Vallens felt that the slogans on the strikers' banners "were very modest," and that the entire meeting had been "rather conservative" in its approach.[4] Nevertheless, on the preceding day Vallens had warned the governor, now reassured by the knowledge that troops were on the scene, that the situation "will be extremely critical. . . . The strikers are aware that they have the Negroes thoroughly frightened and will do everything necessary—even to murder to intimidate them, . . ."[5] Vallens said. The arrest of Sullivan and Driver for the murder of the blackleg Glover and their indictment on May 24 had quieted the strikers down for a few days, but the effect of this was lost when on May 25 the indictment was set aside and the two men were released from custody in what Vallens described as "an outrage on Justice, as the evidence was strong."[6]

The miners' committee charged with enlisting the aid of the railway unions made calls throughout Birmingham on May 28, but with little success. Although the railroad unions were presumably in sympathy with the miners, they were not willing to become involved in the strike. The best answer that the miners could get was that the railroad men had come to no decision.[7]

This result had been anticipated by Vallens, who had told Governor Jones that the coal operators were not afraid that the miners would gain the support of the railroad men.[8] At the same time, it was Detective Foley's opinion that if the miners did fail, the fight would become "more desperate than ever and trouble will follow."[9]

The other committee established as a result of the mass meeting fared as badly as the first one. On May 30, a conference was held in Birmingham between the six miners on the committee and the principal operators. DeBardeleben, Aldrich, and Mc-Cormack represented the Tennessee Company; Seddon and E. W. Rucker sat for the Sloss Company. While the miners and operators held a "considerable discussion" on the state of affairs, the operators would not make any concessions. The miners were informed that the companies were "in a position to carry on their plants regardless of the strike.[10] As the *Labor Advocate* put it, the operators were willing to solve the labor problem by using Negro workers and such white laborers as they could secure.[11]

The strike continued with its previously established pattern of events and actions. For the strikers, the early weeks of June were "trying ones indeed," for more Negroes were imported by the operators and evictions of strikers spread throughout the mining district.[12] Miners at Whitwell, Tennessee, reported that operators from Blossburg had attempted to recruit blacklegs there, and that the reply had been, "We have no blacklegs here, and if we did we would send them somewhere [else] than Alabama to do their work." The press carried almost daily reports of labor importations, of "another bit of negroes brought in," and of mines "almost stocked with negroes."[13] On June 9, the wives and children of the strikers at the Pratt Mines, Negroes and whites, held their own demonstration, marching about the camp carrying a banner protesting the use of blacklegs.[14]

Despite the mounting economic pressure faced by the strikers, there were few defections by the Negro union men. In part their solidarity was achieved through their fear that if they went back to work "they would be killed."[15] Coercion by the whites was certainly present, but it tended to mask the fact that most of the Negroes were as strong in their determination to win the strike as the white miners. When the Sloss Company offered its striking whites and Negroes 45 cents a ton to resume work, both groups rejected the offer although they faced possible eviction.[16] One Negro striker from Coalburg was incensed over the constant references in the press to Negro blacklegs. While visiting the Pratt Mines he discovered that "lo, and behold, all the blacklegs working there were not 'niggers' from the color of their skins at least." As a loyal striker he objected to the popular notion that all blacklegs were Negroes.[17]

As reports were published on coal production it became clear that the operators were succeeding in their basic strategy of using blackleg labor. DeBardeleben had made his major effort at the Blue Creek mines of Adger, Johns, and Sumter, and the production figures helped explain operator intransigence toward any compromise solution to the strike. On May 30, the Blue Creek mines produced 2,330 tons of coal; by June 2, 2,368 tons were being produced; and on June 7, production had risen to 2,496 tons a day.[18] With a constant daily production of about 2,800 tons mined by convict labor, total state production closely paralleled the increases recorded for Blue Creek. On June 2, total production per day stood at 9,405 tons; by June 5, this had been raised to 10,269 tons; and on June 7, production moved upward to 10,732 tons.[19]

Operator success in coal production did nothing to placate the more belligerent miners, intent on harassment and intimidation. A great deal of the trouble resulted from friction between the strikers and company guards, and shots were frequently exchanged between the two groups.[20] The miners, deservedly or not, had enjoyed a bad press on the question of violence. The *Age-Herald* was not alone in its frequent reports of strikers "lurking about in suspicious manner, indicative of intended violence."[21]

This image of the striking coal miners as violent and lawless men was greatly strengthened by the report which the Jefferson County grand jury issued early in June. According to the grand jury, "private citizens standing guard over their property have been threatened, under cover of night, by cowardly men and desperate women with dynamite, poison, fire, gun, and dagger. . . ." Despite the "reason, kindness, and patience" of the operators, "these cutthroats have stamped the mining of coal at thirty cents a ton a capital offense punishable by instant death." To make matters even worse, said the jury, the sheriff and his assistants were hampered and embarrassed by the false sympathy extended "to this class of law breakers by time-servers, office seekers, demagogues, communists and anarchists."[22]

Most of the strikers, though presumably not those actually involved, bitterly resented the charges of violence made against them.[23] A striker from Blossburg, "a Kolb man," reported that when a new group of laborers was brought in they were accompanied by a strong force of deputies and guards "which we supposed was the purpose of protecting their lives and property from the fury of anarchists, murderers, thieves, cutthroats, communists and socialists discovered by the recent Birmingham grand jury." Other miners stated that they had self-respect and were as law-abiding as any citizen in the state. They respected their employers too highly to attempt any such outrages. Many miners were sure that a part of the violence was caused by the guards themselves in an effort to keep their jobs, and by those who desired employment at lucrative guard wages.[24]

Despite their growing economic difficulties and the feeling that they were unjustly persecuted, the miners were still able to wring some humor from the situation. Spoofing the guards and blacklegs, one miner wrote:

> A terrible scare came over the spirit of the mining camp one night last week. James Lelmon while on guard saw a dark object, and after the hair had stood sufficiently straight on his head to push his hat off he fired at what proved to be a shadow and ran into the mines and gave the alarm. All was confusion. George McDonald [a blackleg] bundled his clothes and sobbing piteously said his mama told him not to come. They put out the dogs and only succeeded in treeing two of the guards. So the wicked flee when none pursueth.[25]

The new factor that had entered the strike was the presence of the state troops, busily carrying on their training exercises at Camp Forney. The camp had been located at Ensley, seven miles from Birmingham, "on account of its naturally fine topographical and sanitary conditions; its easy and ready access to every mine and mining camp in the country . . . ; its central location, and readiness and facility with which the camp could be supplied."[26] It had been established with little difficulty, and the three regiments of troops were rotated through it on tours of duty. The second regiment, composed of troops from Birmingham and Bessemer, were the original tenants of Camp Forney. In a send-off editorial, the Bessemer *Weekly* bade the Bessemer Rifles goodby, martially declaring that if "the strikers wish to fight rather than work . . . the opportunity for a test will be offered them."[27] Ironically enough, Lt. Erwin discovered that the local Birmingham band was unionized; he wrote the governor to dispatch a band to Camp Forney.[28] Before the departure of the second regiment on June 4, its cavalry and artillery companies had "shown the flag" at "every mine within several miles of Birmingham."[29]

On June 4, the first regiment reported to Camp Forney, after a farewell from "quite a crowd of the fair sex . . . to encourage them in the path of duty."[30] The first regiment was composed of troops from Mobile, Evergreen, Greenville, and Montgomery. These Black Belt and South Alabama boys felt the alien nature of their industrial surroundings. One trooper from Mobile reported that they were encamped "on a piece of rolling ground, which is studded with a growth of young pines. On either edge is [sic] clumps of hard wood trees, while just to the east is one of the mammouth [sic] iron furnaces that omits [sic] a roaring noise all day long and night."[31] With the red glow of the furnace constantly visible, the troops began to date their letters "Ensley City, near h--l."[32] At Camp Forney everything was carried on under strict discipline, "just as it would be if a battle was expected."[33] There was company drill in the morning and a dress parade every afternoon. It began to seem as if the troops would never get a taste of action.[34]

A release from the tedium of camp life came during the night of June 7, in the seriocomic Battle of Blue Creek. At midnight, Governor Jones, who was in Birmingham, received a telegram from DeBardeleben reporting that 500 armed strikers were in the Blue Creek area and requesting that troops be sent immediately.[35] Governor Jones arranged for an L. & N. train from Birmingham to proceed to Camp Forney and pick up the troops. As the train stopped at the Union Station in Birmingham, DeBardeleben and his son were already aboard. An energetic reporter questioned DeBardeleben about the trouble only to hear him deny knowledge of any trouble anywhere, although it seemed doubtful that he was in the habit of riding special trains at midnight. About 1:00 A.M. the train arrived at Camp Forney and 300 militiamen plus a Gatling gun were loaded on board. Meantime the Birmingham battalion of the second regiment was alerted at midnight and held in readiness at its armory until 2:20 A.M.

The L. & N. train proceeded slowly from Bessemer to Adger, since it was feared that the track would be obstructed. The engine did hit a heavy piece of iron "that came near throwing the train from the tracks."[36] After finally arriving at Adger, the troops were disembarked for a march on the moines with "Governor Jones, Colonel Williams, and Lt. James B. Erwin in front."[37] Instead of armed miners prepared to give battle, the troops discovered only sleepy men, women, and children roused from their rest by the commotion and turmoil. Unwilling for the expedition to end on so painful a note of anticlimax, the troops spent several hours marching around the hills, but the details of the march, with 300 men stumbling and falling in the darkness of those rugged hills and ravines, were mercifully unrecorded.

Governor Jones later claimed that "news of the movement of the troops preceded them, and the mob . . . had dispersed."[38] Although the governor was somewhat crestfallen and admitted that the numbers of the mob were exaggerated, L. W. Johns of the Tennessee Company remained apprehensive. Johns reported that "everybody here was scared up last night, and none of us here have slept a wink, for we expected an attack at any time." He maintained that the strikers "could have outdone us easily last night with the number that were in the woods. We are going to find them if they are here, and if we do, I expect a lively battle."[39]

The Battle of Blue Creek was humorously reported by William Mailley of Adger, who chided the governor for leaving two fence gates open. Mailley added that "some of the cattle we failed to steal, as per the Birmingham grand jury, got in and raised cain among the young corn before your carelessness was discovered."[40]

A similar experience for the troops came on June 12, when it was reported that several hundred armed men planned to destroy the railroad bridge at Chinn's Crossing. There was no question that the destruction of the trestle would effectively interdict coal shipments between Blue Creek and Birmingham, but on their arrival the troops found nothing amiss and returned to camp.[41] The *Labor Advocate* insisted that a fired Negro section hand had sought vengeance against the railroad and was responsible for the attempt to burn Chinn's trestle. Moreover, said the newspaper, the Negro was recognized, shot, and wounded, "yet the daily press heralded it to the world as done by the striking miners, and insolently refuses to correct it."[42] Fired up on its theme of journalistic misrepresentation, the paper added that "when any shooting is done around the mines, and 'mysterious dark forms' are to be seen sneaking around through the night, the sheriff's dogs always tree a deputy. But the pluto [plutocratic] press never tells you one word about this."[43]

Following the abortive troop expeditions, miner sentiment was more openly directed against Governor Jones. When the third regiment relieved the first on June 14, Jones arrived in Birmingham for an extended stay.[44] Some miners argued for a boycott against any business man who employed "a single member of the State troops." The *Labor Advocate* argued that the whole encampment was "an insane policy" that would cost the state $30,000.[45] The more extreme, and often unjustified, trend of miner sentiment was illustrated by the writings of "Courier" from Blocton. Referring to the governor as the "Chief Intimidator," "Courier" wrote:

> from the very beginning of the present strike, he has by his meddlesome conduct, persecuted, intimidated, harassed and annoyed the Miners' Executive Committee. His unsolicited visits to Birmingham, his interviews, threats and proclamations, have been, to say the least, nauseating to the most crude and unlettered of the craft.[46]

State troops rushing about in futile quest of wrongdoers provided some humorous moments, but more serious events were imminent. To offset the success of production by non-union

men the strikers had attempted to gain the support of the railroad workers and shut off the flow of coal. When overtures to
the railway men proved abortive, individual groups of strikers
again took matters into their own hands in an attempt to halt
coal transportation throughout the district. The obvious means
of interdiction was to dynamite or burn the numerous railroad
trestles. If enough of the strategically located bridges could be
put out of commission, no coal would move from the mines
to Birmingham and on to its ultimate markets.

On June 11, Governor Jones offered a reward of $400 for the
capture of those responsible for wrecking a railroad bridge at
Carbon Hill in Walker County.[47] On June 13, Detective Vallens reported that a trestle had been burned west of Cardiff.[48]
Twenty-five men had scared off the guard at the trestle and set
it on fire. The fire was put out, and the bridge repaired with
little disruption of traffic. The railroad companies now began
steps to protect their property. The Louisville & Nashville
brought in a large shipment of rifles and ammunition, and
posted deputized guards on its important bridges.[49] When the
property of the Georgia Pacific Railroad was attacked, the
company, in receivership of Federal court, gained a court order
for fifty United States deputy marshals to guard its property.[50]
Even this protection did not suffice. On June 18, another dynamiting attempt was made on a Georgia Pacific trestle.[51] The
Birmingham *Age-Herald* calculated that an average of one railroad bridge a day was being burned. One of the paper's re-
porters, apparently tired of writing trestle-burning stories,
wearily remarked, "of burning trestles there seems no end."[52]
Intimidation of blackleg labor also continued as more and more
Negroes were brought in. Eight more arrests were made for
participation in the Horse Creek affair, the original violence
of the strike.[53]

At the same time, attempts at a negotiated settlement continued. President Frank Fournier went to Columbus, Ohio,

early in June to confer with President McBride of the national UMW.[54] There he learned that the national strike was almost broken, and that settlements had been authorized on a district basis. The *Age-Herald* optimistically asserted that from now on the Alabama strike would be a "mere desultory struggle here and there," but such a view incorrectly assumed an intimate relationship between the national and the Alabama strikes. With more accurate analysis, the *Age-Herald* added that "it is simply a cold statement of facts to say that any serious and protracted struggle by white mine labor in the South will inevitably lead to its permanent displacement by negroes from the plantations."[55]

On his return from Columbus, President Fournier met with his executive committee. It was decided to attempt an agreement with the operators on the district basis authorized by the national union, and the committee issued an invitation to the operators to meet with it on June 11. If hopes ran high that the strike would soon be brought to an end, they were quickly dashed. Only four small operators attended the meeting. Without the presence of the Tennessee and Sloss companies nothing could be accomplished.[56]

On June 13, the executive committee issued a public statement on its meeting with the operators:

> It is with regret that we acknowledge the failure of the joint conference of miners and operators to arrive at any settlement of our present troubles. We had hopes of a good representation from the operators who wanted to arrange the matter amicably, but . . . they did not materialize, and we are no nearer the goal than before. We are truly thankful to those friendly operators who so willingly responded to our call, and we hope in the near future, with their assistance, we will be able to adjust the matter, and we ask them now to help us to get a sufficient amount of pressure brought to bear on the situation from all sides to at last attain the end desired by the conference.[57]

Feeling that it had exhausted its alternatives, the executive committee believed that the time had now come to place the issues before the rank and file for decision. This seemed to be particularly necessary when news was received that the miners of Pennsylvania and Ohio had signed contracts running from June 18, 1894, to May 1, 1895. In Pennsylvania, where the old scale had paid between 45 and 50 cents per ton, the new agreement provided for a winter scale of 80 cents a ton and a summer scale of 70 cents.[58] Responding to this news, the executive committee called a mass meeting of all strikers to convene at Adamsville on June 18, and "take united action on the present situation."[59]

As the strikers prepared to attend, the state press took a pessimistic and derogatory view of the miners' cause. The Bessemer *Weekly* felt that at the coming meeting "the futility of continuing the strike will probably be recognized, and if not called off it will be understood that success can not be attained and that each one had better look out for himself."[60] The *Age-Herald* accused the miners' executive committee of prolonging the strike, and held it responsible for "the want and hunger which prevails. . . ." According to the paper, "the fight is lost. The men are beaten. . . "[61] The strongest strictures came from the Talladega newspaper, *Our Mountain Home*. The miners had only themselves to blame "for the folly of their selfishness and lawlessness." The paper was convinced that:

> Much of this trouble, if not indeed the fountain source of it, may be traced to that foreign-born element of our society which, absolutely without qualification for the liberties of a free country, has been gradually heaped upon us from the overcrowded, degraded classes of European countries. . . .[62]

The miners fought back through the columns of the *Labor Advocate*, the only local newspaper partisan to their cause. It was observed that when a coal company:

can afford to be so generous, and hire deputies, and import 'scabs,' and place itself in a position to have the militia brought into play as might be supposed for its own benefit, at the expense of the State, they might, if they would poultice their callous consciences and soften their hardened hearts, pay the price the miners ask without a greater expense.[63]

Miner spirits were kept up and correct attitudes inculcated by a special genre of striker poetry. The poem, "The Maiden's Prayer," was a strong indictment with little finesse but considerable fervor, as illustrated by selected stanzas:

> I saw a little maiden
> Upon a Miners' knee,
> Asking for a bite of bread
> And this is what she said:
>
> What will become of Alabama, Pa
> If things go on this way?
> There are hundreds of the colored men
> Scabbing every day.
>
> I hear there's a man in Birmingham,
> Or not very far away,
> Who's trying mighty hard to make
> A Negro Eden pay.
>
> .   .   .   .   .   .
>
> And then there is the grand jury—
> They did not treat us right;
> They called us cutthroats in the day
> And chicken thieves at night.
>
> O, miners, stick, I beg you stick!
> For ours' is a noble fight,
> And the Lord of hosts will help us
> As long as we're in the right.

And do not burn the bridges, boys
Nor wreck a railroad train,
For everything bad that's done
The miners get the blame.

So now, fellow workingmen,
I hope you will keep still:
You might do harm to some innocent man
Who bears us no ill will.[64]

On June 18, at least 800 white and 300 Negro miners assembled at Adamsville to decide the strike's fate.[65] President Fournier called the meeting to order, and announced its purpose as either perfecting organization for a continuance of the strike or deciding on some other course of action. A motion was made to eject from the meeting all who were not miners, and on its passage an *Age-Herald* reporter and "three peanut politicians of the third party religion were driven away."[66] After listening to speeches during the day, the miners reached the point of decision as resolutions were offered and put to a vote. The most important resolution—calling on the miners to stand by the resolution adopted at their earlier Lake View meeting and continue the strike was the first to be offered, and it passed, although the evicted *Age-Herald* reporter maintained that many of the miners wanted to return to work and that "mutterings of disapproval of the first resolution were heard."[67]

Having decided to continue the strike, the miners passed other resolutions to keep material support coming in. They thanked "our colored Brothers" for standing firm, recognized the executive committee as the only bargaining agent, and expressed appreciation to "Adams and his fellow farmers" for making the miners comfortable.[68] Immediately following the formal adjournment of the meeting, they unanimously passed a resolution to support Kolb and the Jeffersonian Democrats in the coming August elections.[69] Economic interest was clarifying political attitudes. Detective Vallens, who was on the outskirts of the Adamsville meeting hoping to pick up information, was informed by a miner that the "Kolb politicians" were anxious for the strikers to remain in their counties (and by implication to continue the strike), "as nearly all the miners in the state are Kolb men" and their leaving the state "would mean a loss of several thousand votes to that party."[70]

If the Jeffersonian Democrats desired the presence of every dissatisfied miner on election day, the mine operators, from political and economic reasons, would be well served if some of the strikers left the state for other jobs. On June 20, DeBardeleben, supported by the Sloss Company, began publication of advertisements offering any miner free transportation to the Northern coal fields. According to DeBardeleben, there were more miners in Alabama than there would ever be jobs; if the strike was settled immediately there would not be enough jobs to go around.[71] Taking into account the hundreds of scabs brought into Alabama and the depressed demand for coal, there was economic accuracy in DeBardeleben's position. But Vallens pointed out that, in addition, "this move on their part is probably one of politics as every miner going away is a vote lost for Kolb."[72]

On the first day of the transportation proposal nearly 100 miners accepted the companies' offer, and it seemed likely that at least 300 to 400 strikers might eventually leave the state.[73] The Labor Advocate maintained that DeBardeleben's transportation policy was adopted to insure Negro laborers a dominant position in the mines.[74]

While the Adamsville meeting had voted to continue the strike until the miners' demands had been met, it was already clear from past actions that the initiative for negotiation was not going to come from the operators. On June 26, the miners' executive committee took the lead in an effort to bring the op-

erators to conference. Union officials made no pretense of trying
to force a state-wide contract with all the operators. This would
have raised the question of union recognition that the operators
were certain to reject and which the union was not prepared to
push. Members from each company could handle the negotiations with their employers. This may have been a realistic approach in the circumstances, but it required iron-clad solidarity
to keep the union front unbroken. In line with this strategy,
the secretary of the executive committee, John G. Smith, wrote
T. H. Aldrich and asked "in your judgment would it not be
wise to call a joint conference of operators and said committee
at an early date."[75] On the following day Aldrich replied that
while there was no organization of the operators, the Tennessee
Company was prepared to speak for itself and was ready to
"meet and treat" with the miners at any time.[76]

On the same day as Aldrich's reply, June 27, a meeting was
arranged among three members of the executive committee (all
on strike against the Tennessee Company) and Nat Baxter,
president of the Tennessee Company, and his assistant general
manager, George B. McCormack.[77] As in earlier meetings, a
long discussion was held between the two sides, but it did nothing to change the basic position of union or company. The
union members stated that they awaited new proposals from
the company. Baxter replied that the strikers could return to
work on the terms originally offered. If they desired their old
jobs back they should apply for them before they were filled
with new workers.[78] The conference ended on the same note of
intransigence already demonstrated by earlier meetings. Strike
pressure on the operators had clearly failed to move the companies to compromise.

If the failure of negotiation meant that the strike would continue into July, there were indications by the end of June that
it would take on a quieter and less violent tone. When the tour
of duty of the third state regiment had expired on June 23,

Governor Jones felt that the situation "though quiet, was not satisfactory."[79] He therefore left a detachment of 250 men at Camp Forney so that force would be at hand if needed. When the next days passed without violence occurring, the governor pulled his remaining troops out of the district and on June 30, the detachment of 250 men left Camp Forney.[80] An uneasy peace now settled over the coal fields.

chapter 6

Trouble at the Tracks

Governor Jones's removal of the state troops from Birmingham on June 30 indicated his hope and expectation that the worst excesses of the strike were past. There were political dangers involved in prolonging the use of the militia, and Jones was genuinely convinced that the troops were no longer needed for the protection of property. A leading figure among the miners, W. J. Kelso, asserted that the governor had "taken his forces off the field, either for campaign purposes or for fear. . . ."[1]

Early in July it was dramatically demonstrated that the governor's hopes for peace were premature. On July 2, a railroad trestle near Adamsville on the Kansas City, Memphis, and Birmingham Railroad was burned, and the watchman and one of his daughters were wounded in an exchange of shots.[2] The *Age-Herald,* incorrectly informed that the affair was one of arson and murder, argued that ways of stopping the violence must be found. "Let us, if necessary," said the paper, "form vigilance

103

committees . . . until these bridge burners and assassins are run to cover and punished as they deserve."[3]

Over 100 Birmingham citizens, acting on the suggestion of the *Age-Herald,* decided to meet again on the following day to consider "practical methods and plans of action."[4] At its next meeting the citizens' group contented itself with asking that the strike come to an end and pledging its intention to see that the laws were enforced.[5] The animus toward the strike shown by the Birmingham citizens' group was one side of public opinion. A citizens' meeting at Oakman, in Walker County showed a different attitude. This assembly protested against the operators because they imported an "inferior element of miners that will retard the progress of the community."[6]

Up to this point in the strike, intimidation of non-union labor and attempts to interdict coal shipments had been the miners' unofficial methods of advancing their cause. Earlier attempts to halt the movement of coal by involving the railroad brotherhoods in the strike had ended in failure.[7] Now, in July, with the strike already entering its third month, it seemed that much-needed reinforcement for the miners' cause might develop.

The hope of the Alabama miners centered in the formation of Eugene V. Debs's American Railroad Union, and the possibility that the new union would call a strike that would effectively stop transportation of coal. Whether a strike by the ARU would affect the coal mine strike depended on the success of the union in organizing Alabama railroad men. During the last week of June, delegates of the ARU were on the scene in Birmingham and were rapidly recruiting new members. On June 30 it was reported that the ARU "is now the strongest single labor organization in the State."[8] Although the claimed membership of the ARU in Alabama was only 1,400, and thus far smaller than the miners' union, its members were concentrated in the Birmingham district. The railway union met with much

less success in Mobile and Montgomery, and Montgomery railroad employees adopted a resolution disapproving of the union
and its sympathy strike called by Debs in support of the Pullman Company strikers in South Chicago.[9]

For a short time the Pullman strike seemed removed and re-
mote from Alabama, but as it swiftly spread through the ARU,
immediacy took the place of remoteness.[10] On July 6 yard-
workers on the Louisville & Nashville and Kansas City, Memphis, and Birmingham quit work. Firemen on the Queen and
Crescent Railroad left their jobs and refused to pull any cars
except those carrying United States mail.[11] By July 7 the railroad strike was complete in Birmingham, and since Birmingham was the rail center of the mining district, the ARU strike
promised to accomplish what weeks of railroad trestle burning
had failed to do. The operators' inability to ship their coal
would give the miners a needed weapon of economic leverage.
The strike might yet be won.

Miners were given little time to savor the optimistic situation.
On July 7, Governor Jones, feeling that the ARU strike had
little justification, issued a proclamation denouncing the "folly
and wickedness of attempting to interrupt the use of our rail-
ways, and bring harm upon the whole people. . . ."[12] The governor followed his words with action. Because Camp Forney
had been closed, he had, before the ARU strike reached Alabama, instructed Lt. Erwin to "look around for good camp
ground near Birmingham for about eight hundred men and
make preliminary engagements for it."[13] Erwin found a site on
Avenue A in Birmingham, and the governor, after making his
public proclamation against the strike on July 7, issued "cau-
tionary orders to the state troops." Preparations were made to
"afford strong and prompt support of the civil authorities."[14]
By July 22, troops had been stationed at both Camp Forney
and Avenue A.[15]

On July 8, the ARU strikers gathered in the Birmingham

Union Station in such numbers that the movement of trains became physically difficult. The strikers were joined by curious sightseers who watched the strikers' committees meet each train on its arrival at the station. The committees, "by persuasion and threats," sought to induce the trainmen to leave their posts, and they met with some success.[16] Quarrels and altercations resulted, "while the vast throng looked on, jeered and yelled, and hourly became more disorderly and reckless."[17] Governor Jones learned that the Birmingham police force was too small to clear the station and that few deputies could be spared from their guard duty at the coal mines and trestles. He felt that "any attempt by his small force" to remove the strikers, "especially if blood was shed" would have led to "general bloodshed and destruction of property."[18] Lt. Erwin later commented, "Strange to say there seemed a lack of co-operation between the striking miners and railroad men, and it was not until the railroad strike was virtually settled, that the striking miners again began deviltry."[19]

Arriving in Birmingham at midnight on July 8, Governor Jones held hasty conferences with Sheriff Morrow and with the acting mayor. The mayor certified that troops were needed to protect property, and Governor Jones immediately issued orders calling the entire first regiment plus the Montgomery battalion of the second regiment into action.[20]

On the morning of July 9, the Birmingham troops cleared the station of all strikers, and peace and quiet greeted the 600 troops when they arrived at noon.[21] During the next week, troops were used to guard and regulate the passenger station and its approaches. They broke up demonstrations so that trains could run on schedule, and roundhouses and other railroad property were guarded. By July 11 the railroad strike was broken. In many instances strikers who sought to return to their jobs were not rehired. The Birmingham local of the Brotherhood of Locomotive Firemen, which had refused to join the strike, declared that firemen who had quit work were subject to dismissal from the Brotherhood.[22] With one massive stroke of intervention Governor Jones had broken the ARU strike, although he gave considerable credit to public opinion for the victory.

The Union Springs *Herald* approved of the actions taken by both President Cleveland and Governor Jones to break the strike: "The public highways must be kept open, the mails must move, life must be preserved, and the government must be protected...."[23] *Our Mountain Home* of Talladega argued that the railroad strike had "degenerated into anarchy" and that there was "no excuse under Heaven for the course pursued by the striking railroad men."[24] Farther afield, Governor Jones's actions excited the admiration of the Washington *Post:*

> We infer that the South is not yet ready for the kind of social and political reform which Beckmann and Schwab have been preaching, and which Altgeld and Debs have endeavored to promote. Let us hope that Governor Jones will act with vigor and precision. Perhaps if he shows us how to deal with conspirators in Alabama the lesson may be applied in other states and finally in all of them.[25]

The railroad employees had no powerful agency to speak for them. Their side of the question was rarely presented and but faintly heard. The Birmingham Trades Council gave its support to the ARU strike, and condemned Governor Jones for calling out the troops "before any law had been violated."[26] An Alabama coal miner bluntly interpreted the strike as having been caused by "that d----d Pullman who is starving his employees."[27] The miner's description differed but slightly from that of Debs himself who claimed that Pullman was "as heartless as a stone, as remorseless as a savage and as unpitying as an incarnate fiend."[28]

Few elements of the Alabama press took the broad analytical view of the Montgomery *Journal:*

The social unrest throughout the country is shown, not so much by the Pullman Strike, as by the sympathetic strikes that have followed. . . . The unrest is due to the stringency of the times, the scarcity of money, the poverty of the masses, and the increasing wealth of the classes, to the enforced idleness of hundreds of thousands of people willing to work and to the real or imaginary tyranny of capital.

To call out the military, to have troops stationed at every available point throughout the country . . . is a temporary expedient, and will arrest the dangers of the present; but in a free country, an armed constabulary to maintain law and order, with a standing army stationed in the principal cities . . . is an anomalous condition which can not long exist. There must be some other solution. That solution is neither a standing army nor the single gold standard.[29]

With the railroad strike in Birmingham broken, the miners again resumed the full burden of labor protest. Under the attribution of time and the operators' counterattack, the hitherto unbroken front of the state-wide strike began to weaken and crumble. On July 7 the miners in Walker County agreed to return to work.[30] They had originally joined the strike in sympathy with the miners of the Tennessee Company, but the bonds of labor solidarity had now been stretched past the breaking point. Their defection, deliberately ignored by the *Labor Advocate,* was nonetheless a serious psychological blow to the miners' cause. The Tennessee and Sloss miners still stood firm, but a flaw in the united front had been revealed. It could be expected that the operators would attempt to use the new situation to their advantage.

On July 11, DeBardeleben met with the miners' executive committee and offered a new set of propositions. Since the operators had been unwilling to go beyond their original offer in earlier talks, the new proposals were evidence that the operators were now willing to bargain. DeBardeleben offered the same 35 cents a ton scale, but he introduced a new element by proposing that mining wages be directly tied to the price received by the companies for Number 3 foundry iron. The De-Bardeleben scale provided: 35 cents a ton to be paid when iron netted the company $7.00 or less a ton; a 2½ cent a ton increase in wages for every increase of 50 cents netted for iron. To soften the sting to the miners of returning to work at the despised 35 cents a ton, DeBardeleben also offered to pay them cash on a bi-monthly basis. Although his 35 cent a ton offer applied to the Pratt and Blocton mines, Blue Creek miners were to receive only 30 cents.[31] The *Age-Herald* characterized DeBardeleben's offer as "a slightly better proposition than the company has been standing on," and it felt that the offer of cash wages was a "very good peg on which to hang a compromise."[32]

The offer to pay wages in cash appealed to the strikers, but the promise of the DeBardeleben scale depended on a return of good times and an advance in iron prices. Prior to the Panic of 1893, miners had made 45 cents a ton with iron selling for $13 a ton. Under the DeBardeleben scale a return of iron prices to $13 would have raised miners' wages to 65 cents per ton. With the pall of depression still around them they were faced with the necessity of deciding.

On July 12, the strikers held meetings at the various mines and elected delegates to represent them in a meeting planned for the following day. The convention that met in Birmingham grappled with the alternatives of a disappointing present and a happier future. By a "practically unanimous vote" it took its stand. In belligerent style the convention decided to adhere to the Adamsville resolutions on wages and to reject the offer of the Tennessee Company. No further conventions were to be called until the wage demands of the strikers had been met. The determination of the miners to continue the strike seemed unweakened by privation, by the breaking of the railroad strike, or by the defection of the miners of Walker County. Despite its

bold words, the convention took one other action. It empowered
the executive committee to negotiate a settlement with all companies *except* the Tennessee and Sloss concerns. With this action the union brought its policies into line with the reality of
the Walker County desertion. The strike, as an official state-
wide action by the union, had come to an end.[33]

On July 14 the miners' executive committee made formal announcement of the union's new policy. Claiming that "the suspension now indicates that our victory is assured," the committee declared the strike at an end for all mines "where operators
are willing, and arrange to pay the price that was in effect previous to April 14, 1894."[34] The union now attempted to use the
same divide and conquer tactics employed by the operators.

In retrospect, the events of July 11-14 marked a fundamental
turning point in the coal mine strike. However, to the men of
that day there was little reason to think that the tribulations
of the strike lay behind them. The strike had crested, but the
wave of unrest had yet to break.

Since Governor Jones had sent troops into Birmingham on
July 9 all had been peaceful in the coal mining communities.
Intimidation of the blacklegs and attempts to burn railroad
bridges had ceased as the miners followed the negotiations with
the Tennessee Company. On July 16 Governor Jones ordered
the state troops relieved from duty, and they began their departure from Birmingham. About 4:30 P.M., not more than two
hours after the troops had left the city, violence erupted at
Slope 3 of the Pratt Mines. At 5:40 Sheriff Morrow received an
urgent telegram from Jones G. Moore, superintendent of the
Pratt Mines. Moore wired: "Send deputies and troops. Strikers
are killing my negroes at Slope No. 3."[35]

Testimony taken later showed that on the morning of July
16 a group of miners (estimates ranged from forty to three
hundred) had met at Village Creek to "devise some way of
getting rid of the negro miners who had taken their places. . . ."[36]
The miners' plans were later revealed by a striker who was

injured and captured by deputies. The *Age-Herald* reported him to be a Frenchman named Racquet; the Mobile *Daily News* agreed that he was French but gave his name as Laflure. According to his story, W. J. Kelso, who served as the union's regular correspondent to the *United Mine Workers Journal,* presided over the meeting, during the course of which the men planned an attack on the workers at the Pratt mines. Both Negroes and whites were to participate. The strikers gathered at the entrance of Slope 3 and waited until the fifty or sixty Negro blacklegs finished their work and emerged from the mine. When the blacklegs reached the surface, the strikers opened fire, three blacklegs and one company guard being killed in the fusillade. There was good reason for the warning telegram to Sheriff Morrow.[37]

Governor Jones, who had remained in Birmingham, was immediately notified of Moore's message, and again the chief executive swung into action. Lt. Erwin and a small guard force that had remained in camp were dispatched to the scene at once, and Col. L. V. Clark and his Birmingham battalion of state troops followed. The governor issued orders recalling the departing state troops. Their trains were turned around, and as darkness came they began to arrive in Birmingham.[38] Governor Jones believed that acts of incendiarism in Birmingham had occurred simultaneously with the violence at the Pratt Mines, and that these actions were a "general combination on the part of the vicious elements to engage in . . . violence. . . ."[39] Although the local press had not reported fires as being set by strikers, the *Age-Herald* on July 22 told of the rumor that the miners "planned to burn Birmingham." Lt. Erwin had it as: "interference with railroad property; attempts at incendiarism and demonstrations at other mines."[40] Soldiers armed with shotguns were stationed at the slopes of the Pratt Mines and in the city with orders to shoot "whenever there is the slightest justification."[41]

Three days after the "Pratt Massacre" seventy-nine miners

had been arrested and charged with murder, and deputies with warrants continued to search for twenty-five other strikers.[42] A visitor to the Jefferson County jail, which was soon full of arrested miners, reported:

> All the while a perfect jabber of French and Welsh, Scotch and British was kept up between the prisoners and their wives as they caught glimpses of one another. A man could stand by for half an hour without hearing any good, old fashioned Alabama accent. One might have closed his eyes and imagined himself very far from the South, so far as the tongues of the prisoners and their wives would indicate.[43]

While the violence at the Pratt Mines had the desired effect of intimidating blackleg labor—non-union men at Blue Creek quit work for a few days under threats that they would be killed —at the same time it intensified the already bitter opinion toward the miners' cause.[44] The strike and the miners were now the subject of unrestrained attacks by the state press. The Mobile *Daily News* characterized the strikers as "perfectly fiendish, their malice only equalled by their cowardice."[45] The Jacksonville *Republican* called the murders at the Pratt Mines the "most brutal and cowardly act in the annals of crime in Alabama," and claimed that the guilty parties were "those Huns, Poles, and other outlandish fellows who are causing this disturbance."[46] The Bessemer *Weekly* declared that the past few months had been "a history of a succession of outrages and lawlessness," and that violence had now "culminated in one of the most cowardly massacres of inoffensive men that fiends in human shape can be guilty of. . . ."[47] While the *Age-Herald* referred to the "unholy strike" and "murderous deeds,"[48] it realized, with considerable insight, the uniqueness of the coal strike. After pointing out the resort to violence in northern coal fields, the *Age-Herald* added: "The situation here is abnormal and peculiar in the South, occurring only once in a life time, and therefore creates abnormal alarm and uneasiness. In the older mining regions similar situations are exceedingly common."[49]

Citizens of Birmingham, sure that a crisis of violence was upon them, again took steps to uphold law and order. A "Committee of Twenty-Five" was established to organize reserve forces of armed civilians. One such group was the Mounted Rifle Club, strikingly attired in black hats, blue blouses, gray pants, tan leggings, and yellow handkerchiefs worn around the neck.[50] Meetings denouncing the Pratt Massacre were held in Elyton, Pratt City, and Birmingham. During the Birmingham meeting all businessmen were requested to stop contributing to striker relief.[51]

The *Labor Advocate*, denounced by the conservative press as a "firebrand in the hands of the lawless," vigorously condemned the resort to violence. The editor pointed out that the "condition of many of us is fearful in the extreme, but violence and rebellion will not bring prosperity."[52] He argued that the miners should have put themselves under military discipline, which "would have prevented the Horse Creek trouble, saved the lives of those who have fallen at Pratt City, and won the respect of the world. . . ."[53]

Governor Jones had strong support among the state's conservatives for his actions in using the state troops against the miners and the railroad workers. Yet there were grumbles of disapproval. Not only would use of the troops be employed as a political weapon against the Bourbons, but the long tours of duty were not appreciated by the state troops. Speaking for the Escambia County soldiers, one writer commented that the governor's last call to arms "went decidely against the grain" since the "boys have had quite enough of camp life."[54]

The governor's exasperation was clear when he requested a meeting with the miners' executive committee on July 19. Lt. Erwin sitting with him, Jones informed the union officials in-

cluding President Fournier, John LaMont, John Bell, and John
Stich, that he would hold them responsible if they stood "further in the way of the free and unconstrained exercise by every
miner in Alabama of his individual right to determine himself
what he ought to do in settling this strike."[55] Much earlier in the
strike Governor Jones' policy had won the support of the operators.[56] Now he specifically told the miners that "this lawlessness began with the strike, and will continue . . . as long as the
strike continues."[57] Jones was undoubtedly sincere when he
asked the executive committee to rescind its strike order and
let every miner decide his own course of action. Yet agreement
by the committee would have meant renouncing a basic tenet
of unionism. The executive committee explained to the governor that there were certain elements among the miners that
it could not control, and that he overestimated the committee's
power and authority. Specifically, the committee did not have
the authority to call off the strike. Without instruction from
the membership the strike would continue.[58]

Unable to force the executive committee to end the strike,
Governor Jones moved to a closer alliance with the operators.
Throughout the strike DeBardeleben and the Tennessee Company had concentrated their attack on the company's Blue
Creek and Pratt mines. No effort had been made to evict strikers from their homes at Blocton, or to bring in blacklegs to
work the mines. Blocton had remained in a state of tranquil
truce. Now in July it became clear that the Tennessee Company
had decided to increase pressure on the Blocton strikers. On
July 8, the governor sent a detachment of troops into Blocton
because of a reported demonstration. The alarm proved false,
and the presence of troops brought a spirited rejoinder from
influential citizens of Blocton:

We call upon the conservative and liberty loving citizens of
Alabama to unite with us in some action to restrain the military

mad governor in his unwarranted usurpation of authority, in this, throwing troops into the midst of a peaceable and law-abiding people for no other purpose than to harass and annoy its citizens.[59]

Additional pressure was soon placed on the Blocton miners. On July 21, the Tennessee Company ordered the strikers to vacate all company houses within ten days or suffer eviction.[60] On July 23, Governor Jones conferred with the strikers at Blocton. When the miners explained why they could not accept the company's offer, the governor admitted that he had no power to decide the merits of the controversy but stated that "in view of the hopelessness of the strike and the fact that its continuance meant lawlessness" he had hoped the strikers would return to work. Although the miners might decline to call off the strike, he would be forced "to protect other laborers" who desired to work.[61] The Blocton miners had the situation made clear to them: if they refused to return to work it seemed probable that the company, supported by the state, would reopen the mines with non-union labor. Despite this threat a Negro member of the Blocton miners committee vigorously denied an item in the Birmingham *Evening News* quoting him as favoring a return to work at 35 cents a ton.[62]

On July 23, Governor Jones publicly announced that troops would remain on duty in the coal fields until the strike came to an end. On July 25, Sheriff Morrow certified that troops were needed to maintain the peace at least for two more weeks.[63]

The violence of the railroad strike and the Pratt Massacre brought a renewed surge of activity by the Pinkerton detectives. The two investigators known as "E. W." and "J. M. P." were particularly active during July and early August. Both detectives were from Chicago, and "J. M. P." posed as a labor reporter from the Chicago *Workman* in an attempt to win the miners' trust. The detectives obtained most of their information by lounging in Pratt City and Birmingham saloons and buying drinks and cigars for the idle miners. Among the bars they frequented were the Ruby Saloon, Brown's Saloon, Marble Saloon, Bank Saloon, McDonald's Saloon, Wilson's Saloon, and Fox's Saloon, as well as the Outlaw, New Acme, White Elephant, and Pratt City Exchange.

The agents dutifully passed on their findings to Lt. Erwin and Governor Jones, although their information was often of doubtful value. "E. W." advised retention of the troops while reporting that too many of the soldiers drank on duty and "two of the regulars being intoxicated sat down and fell asleep by the track near Ensley."[64] It is doubtful if many strikers accepted the detectives in their assumed roles. "E. W." reported that he visited a Scotch settlement near Blossburg and found sixteen miners engaged in the peaceful occupation of pitching quoits (probably horseshoes). "I got no information from them," he wrote. "I think they regard me with suspicion and they are not [at all] friendly toward a stranger."[65]

With Pinkerton detectives and soldiers on hand to warn and guard against further violence; with preliminary hearings in progress against miners charged with the Pratt Massacre; with the railroad strike crushed and the Walker County miners going back to work; the miners' strike was greatly reduced in strength and influence. But after a duration of almost four months, it still continued with a measure of effectiveness. The Blue Creek mines were not working at full capacity, and the Pratt Mines managed full production only through the use of convict labor. No miners were working at the Blocton mines. The Sloss Company had managed to bring in from three to four hundred blacklegs to man its mines at Coalburg, Blossburg, Brookside, and Cardiff, but production was far below its pre-strike norms.[66] Although seriously weakened the strikers were still not defeated.

While it was obvious that the economic depression was the

immediate cause of the strike, the state's political situation had from the first played a major role. The strikers had much to gain by deferring any settlement until the outcome of the gubernatorial election on August 8. If Reuben F. Kolb, the Jeffersonian Democratic candidate, defeated Bourbon Democrat William C. Oates, the miners could expect a more congenial climate of opinion toward their cause and perhaps a drastic re-orientation of the role played by the state government. As August approached, the attention of the miners turned to politics and the political campaign that was in progress. There was little doubt where the sentiments of labor lay.

chapter 7

The Miners
and Political Protest

In 1892 the monolithic structure of Alabama's Democratic Party had been shattered. Reuben F. Kolb's agrarian followers, finding it impossible to capture control of the Democratic Party from its Bourbon leaders, had organized as a separate party, and Kolb and Jones had battled for the governorship in a vigorous and vituperative campaign. Jones's opponents claimed that he was re-elected because his followers resorted to fraud and chicanery in a manipulation of the Black Belt vote.[1] Despite a background of labor political agitation, the coal miners did not play an organized role in the campaign of 1892. They were attracted by the Jeffersonian promise to remove the convicts from the mines, but the subtle interplay of economics and politics had not yet created a cohesive miner political orientation.

But by 1893 the ferment of political revolt had strongly affected the coal miners. In belligerent fashion they raised the issue of convict labor, and Governor Jones's promise of eventual removal of the convicts did not allay their demands for immediate action. The Panic of 1893 was the conclusive determinant of miner political attitudes. Depression and its corollary of wage reductions resulted in the organization of the United Mine Workers of Alabama, unionization making possible the strike of 1894. A sharpened political animosity resulted from the abrasive action of economic want and suffering. As the Jeffersonians and Bourbons prepared to continue their battle in 1894, the coal miners' strike became a central issue of the political campaign.

Jeffersonian Democrats and Populists approached the campaign of 1894 with bitter memories of past injustices. One unhappy agrarian wrote:

> . . . what a miserable and gloomy state of affairs in Alabama! A state house filled with men who were never elected! A press accessory to this enormity! A pulpit silent in the midst of such iniquity! A large majority of white men run over, brow beaten, and insulted by an insolent minority! The state doubly disgraced; first, that any set of men would perpetrate such outrages; second, that such outrages are submitted to.[2]

If the past brought frustration and bitterness, the future seemed to hold out greater opportunities for the reform cause. The Bourbon candidate most frequently mentioned to succeed Governor Jones was William G. Oates, an implacable enemy of the Farmers' Alliance. Oates's conservatism was so pronounced that his candidacy foreshadowed a schism in the ranks of the Democrats. He respected and supported President Cleveland, despite the latter's unpopularity in Alabama, and opposed free silver despite its endorsement by the Democratic state convention of 1892.[3]

The Jeffersonians and the Populists were the first to organize for political battle. In an effort to assure co-operation and coordination during the campaign, both parties called conventions for February 1894 in Birmingham. Meetings were held throughout the state and over twelve hundred delegates from sixty-three counties were selected.[4]

The Populists and Jeffersonians held separate and joint convention sessions with Republican leaders present as observers. On the morning of February 8, the Populists met and appointed a state executive committee, adopted a platform, and endorsed Kolb for governor. In the afternoon a joint session was held with the Jeffersonians. In an atmosphere of fervor and enthusiasm Kolb was nominated for governor and candidates for various state offices were named.[5] The Jeffersonian platform declared for a free vote with an honest count, a contest law for state elections, and the free coinage of silver at a ratio of sixteen to one. In direct appeal for miners' votes and in an effort to capitalize on widespread labor unrest, the Jeffersonian platform called for the removal of convicts from the mines, lien laws for miners, a state inspector of weights and measures, election of mine inspectors, and the prohibition of children under thirteen from working in the mines.[6] In a convention aside, so to speak, William Stevens, Negro Black and Tan Republican was ejected from the hall, a step which may have been taken in an effort to retain the support of the Republican Lily Whites.[7]

Though supporting the same candidates, the Jeffersonians and Populists retained their separate organizations—at times with great difficulty.[8] As these reform groups threw down the gage of battle to their Bourbon opponents, the coal miners were already experiencing "the cold wave of reduction."[9] The United Mine Workers of Alabama was conducting strikes at the Dolomite and Mary Lee mines. Union men had seen their income steadily decline,[10] and in these circumstances the Jeffersonian appeal to the miners received an immediate and massive response. On February 28, representatives of 10,000 miners caucused in Birmingham to determine their course of action in the political campaign. Kolb's nomination and the Jeffersonian platform were endorsed. The miners nominated their own candidates for the state legislature to run on the Kolb ticket.[11] Thus, more than a month before the coal mine strike added its issues and bitterness to the campaign, the miners had aligned themselves with Kolb and the cause of reform.

The regular Democrats not only faced the realities of Jeffersonian opposition, but were troubled by party dissension between gold and silver advocates. Joseph F. Johnston, Birmingham banker and promoter, declared for free silver and announced his intention to seek the Democratic nomination for governor.[12] In late January, Oates declared that at the urging of Governor Jones and others, he too would seek the nomination.[13] After a vigorous fight by the two men, the state Democratic convention nominated Oates by the close vote of 271 to 233.[14] Johnston charged that he had been cheated out of the nomination, and vented his anger in an attack on the pro-Oates Montgomery *Advertiser*.[15]

While Oates was an experienced campaigner (and his empty sleeve was a dramatic reminder of his Civil War service), his political liabilities were considerable. His support of President Cleveland and his Bourbon record of opposition to certain reform measures were open targets for attack.[16] He was also bound by the policies and actions of Governor Jones. By its very magnitude the coal mine strike would have been a major political issue, but the governor's active role threw it into the center of the campaign melee.

The Jeffersonian demand that convicts be removed from the mines was a strong inducement for miner support, but the issue received less emphasis in the actual campaign than in earlier contests.[17] Jeffersonians and Bourbons agreed on a policy of removing the convicts, and were opposed only on the question of immediate versus a slow and planned withdrawal. Despite the agreement on principle, the Jeffersonians were attacked on the issue with ridicule and sarcasm. The conservative Selma *Times* hypothesized that "if Captain Kolb and Governor he would turn the last convict loose to pick blackberries and rob hen-roosts for a living—to make room for skilled dynamiters and mine burners, most of whom are riff-raffs from Europe."[18]

The issues of the strike soon overshadowed the long-standing question of convict labor. Governor Jones's use of the state militia was sharply attacked by the Jeffersonians and staunchly defended by his Bourbon supporters. Peyton Bowman, chairman of the Jeffersonian executive committee, declared that "if this thing continues every plowman in this part of the state will be followed by a soldier with his bayonet."[19] The Bourbon press retorted that the Jeffersonian executive committee "practically and in effect endorse the burning of railroad and other property in the mineral district."[20] When William H. Skaggs, chairman of the Jeffersonian and Populist central compaign committee, argued that Governor Jones had exceeded his authority in ordering out the state troops, the *Age-Herald* observed that since Skaggs, "the most respectable of all the leaders of the polyglot party," advocated dynamiting and arson what could be expected from those "that gallop just behind him!"[21] The Columbia *People's Advocate* retorted that Jones, "the Governor de facto," was "doing everything in his power to bring a collision between the striking miners and the military," but to the credit of the miners he had been unsuccessful.[22]

The Bourbon press followed the strategy of equating any defense of the miners with advocacy of violence and anarchy. Such an approach was premised on the inference of Jeffersonian leaders that Kolb would not have used state troops in the strike.[23] The Union Springs *Herald* maintained that no one had the right to interfere with property or to prevent others from working. "It is this," argued the paper, "that the populists . . . seem to favor—at least they are strongly in sympathy

with the strikers who are doing this kind of thing."[24] Warming
to its theme, the newspaper continued:

> What do you suppose would have been the condition of things
> in Alabama now if the Kolbites had had control of the govern-
> ment during the miners' strike? They endorse the miners and the
> miners endorse them. With such mutual affection and sympathy
> and fellow feeling between the two is it reasonable to suppose
> that Governor Kolb would have ordered the state troops in camp
> at Birmingham to preserve order, enforce the law, and protect
> the rights and property of citizens . . . ? Will anyone dare answer
> the querry [sic] affirmatively? We doubt it. Rather isn't it more
> reasonable to suppose . . . that Kolb like his brother Populite
> Governor Waite, of Colorado, would draw the miners under the
> protecting care of his high office and keep the violators of law
> in secret hiding from the officers in search of them? Governor
> Waite did that. Could we reasonably expect less of Kolb?[25]

Other newspapers reiterated the theme: as long as a conservative Democrat was governor "anarchy and lawlessness"[26] would
not hold sway. "Anarchy shall not flourish its red flag or gory
head in Alabama."[27]

In the midst of charge and countercharge one observer was
apprehensive about the portent and meaning of the times. Em-
mett O'Neal, the young United States attorney for the northern
district of Alabama, argued that "the government has inter-
posed in a conflict between men and dollars . . . ; what was a
'strike' may even now be revolution." O'Neal pointed out that
the people were "no longer controllable by the arts and methods
of machine politics and may not much longer be amenable to
the dictates of reason and judgment." The "righteous resent-
ment of a wronged people" might at any time descend on their
capitalist oppressors. O'Neal, who would, ironically enough,
later be elected governor as the candidate of the conservative
faction of the Democratic Party, believed at this time that a
crisis was imminent in Alabama and strongly opposed the use

of state troops by Governor Jones. In a letter to Senator John
Tyler Morgan, O'Neal said that he regretted that his attempts
to warn the Bourbons that their policies would lead to their
own destruction had earned him "only the honorable appella-
tion of 'crank' . . . ; now I can neither serve nor save those who
have wantonly played with the fire that is to consume and destroy them root and branch."[28] He felt that the coal mine strike
had resulted from the efforts of the operators to replace white
miners with more subservient Negro workers.[29]

Although O'Neal saw the economic struggle that threatened
to rend the fabric of society, he misjudged Bourbon weakness
in the face of popular revolt. The basic economic issues of the
day were never argued and discussed in the political campaign.
The plight of the farmer, the condition of labor, and the
diarchy of business and government were not the issues presented by the Bourbons. Conservatives appealed for support on
the grounds that "it is Kolb's friends that burn bridges, who
killed a man who was guarding a bridge, and who cruelly shot
his two little girls." By making the election turn on emotional
issues, they hoped to outmaneuver their opponents. One Democrat wrote, "The leaders of the Kolb party are well wishers to
the burning of bridges—killing the guards, killing little innocent girls and destroying private property."[30]

For the first time in an election the conservatives faced the
organized opposition of the coal miners. In 1892, Jefferson
County had been carried for Jones by a majority of almost 3,000
votes. In 1894, with labor sentiment militantly arrayed against
the Bourbons, Kolb's chances of carrying the populous county
seemed greatly improved. It was this situation, the Kolb supporters later charged, that prompted the Tennessee and Sloss
companies to announce on June 20, that they would pay the
cost of transportation for any miner who wished to leave the
state.[31] One Kolb newspaper placed little credence in De-
Bardeleben's explanation that the companies were attempting

to solve the over supply of labor. The Tuscaloosa *Journal* contended:

> DeBardeleben's little game of free transportation to the Ohio district for striking miners will deceive no one. Those miners will vote the Jeffersonian ticket to a man, hence Mr. DeBardeleben's generosity. The object is to get Kolb supporters out of the State before the August election. There is no doubt but these men would pledge to support the organized ticket in the August election.[32]

Estimates assumed that at least three or four hundred strikers would leave the state prior to the election, but it is not possible to determine precisely how successful the policy actually was.

The Negro vote was of prime importance to Jeffersonians and Bourbons. The Jeffersonians, recalling charges of Black Belt manipulation of the Negro vote, predicted that the same tactics would again be used against them. One Kolb editor advised that "the best thing for the negro voter to do in the coming registration and election is to keep hands off and let the white voters settle the matter between themselves."[33] Nominal control of the Negro vote was in the hands of the Republicans. William Stevens, offended by his treatment at the Jeffersonian convention, had thrown his support to Oates. N. A. Mosely, head of the Lily White faction that contained both whites and Negroes, supported Kolb. The Republicans issued a circular, signed by Mosely, urging Negroes not to register or vote. Mosely's position was that it would be harder for the Bourbons to manufacture votes that had not been cast than to change votes cast against them, but the strategy was unsuccessful in the end.[34]

The Jeffersonians openly sought the Negro vote, but the coal mine strike provided potent ammunition for the Bourbons. The policy of the coal mine operators in hiring Negro blackleg labor was interpreted as a sign of Bourbon sympathy and aid to the Negro; the strikers' antipathy and resort to violence against such laborers was presented as evidence of the anti-Negro sentiment of the Jeffersonians. Following the Pratt Massacre, one conservative editor declared that "we now think it is a foregone conclusion that every registered negro in the black belt and the great majority in Alabama will cast their votes for Colonel Oates. . . ."[35] "Sam Slim," in a direct appeal for Negro votes, wrote:

> And you colored Republican voters, what do you think of a party that not only kicks your chairman [Stevens] out of the convention, but shoots down your fellows to prevent them from working for an honest living? Suppose you go to the mines to work? It is your right and privilege [sic] to do so. Why, you would be shot unless Gov. Jones who is a democrat, kept troops there to protect you. Who will you vote for? The party that protects you while you work, or the party that shoots you for working to feed your wives and children?[36]

On the eve of the election the New York *Times* surveyed the situation in Alabama and declared that Oates would win. Governor Jones's action in calling out the state troops "has made a profound impression upon the intelligent negroes everywhere, and the kind and manly conduct of Mr. H. F. DeBardeleben . . . has been an object lesson to them they can understand."[37] Bourbon appeals undoubtedly made an impression on some Negro voters, but when the Republican convention met at Centreville on July 21, it endorsed Kolb for governor.[38] The campaign was noteworthy for its tangled political alignments. William F. Aldrich, a Republican and the owner of the Montevallo mines, ran for Congress as a fusion candidate with strong Jeffersonian support.[39] His more renowned brother, Truman H. Aldrich, resigned his position as general manager of the Tennessee Company and ran for Congress from the Ninth District.[40]

For the miners the political campaign became an inextricable part of their strike. The saloons of Pratt City and Birmingham were full of miners who "have completely forgotten the strike and think of nothing but politics." In their discussions "their main topic of conversation was Kolb."[41] Miner passions ran high, and one Pinkerton detective reported that he "would not be surprised if there was trouble after the election should Kolb be elected as they [the strikers] will then think they will be protected in anything they may do. Again should Oates be elected that may make them worse and they will try vengeance."[42]

Most of the miners took no direct part in the campaign, but two strikers became involved in a minor *cause celebre*. Two men whose last names were Fairley and Hannegan solicited funds throughout the South for support of the strike. During their travels they attended a Democratic meeting in Columbus, Georgia, at which Oates was speaking. Fairley reported that he had replied to Oates' attack on the miners. "I was cheered to the echo and have killed his chances of election in this end of the state."[43] The account of the incident in the conservative press, however, put a different light on Fairley's forensic abilities. According to these newspapers a little bald-headed, red-faced man, "whose broken English showed that he was a foreigner," began an attack on Governor Jones and the Democratic party. Fairley was quoted, in strange dialect, as stating that "if you elect Ternal Oats dovernor de Niggers will take Minchesters and murder de miners and make prostitutes uv dare wives and daughters."[44] The meeting broke up in pandemonium. Ladies rushed for the doors, "indignant men sprang towards the speaker to resent the outrageous language." Fairley and his companion were driven from the meeting.[45] The *Labor Advocate,* which had quoted a Democratic version of the incident commented: "The public is thus given another illustration of how facts are colored and distorted to suit certain purposes."[46]

Governor Jones feared that the passions of the strike would manifest themselves on election day. He gave careful orders to Lt. Erwin for the state troops to be kept in camp; troops lounging around the polls would revive memories of Reconstruction elections. If disturbances occurred on election day, the governor wanted to await an appeal from Sheriff Morrow "before taking any part for the preservation of the peace." If there was danger of an attack "disconnected with the election, you will have to act as circumstances require."[47]

The election proceeded without the violence feared by Governor Jones. At face value the returns were conclusive. Out of the 194,167 votes cast, Oates received 110,875 to Kolb's 83,292—an Oates plurality of 27,583.[48] Despite the turmoil of the campaign the vote in 1894 was smaller than that of 1892. Oates's victory was the product of tremendous majorities given him in the counties of the Black Belt. Out of the 6,684 voters in Dallas County, 6,517 apparently voted for Oates. In Wilcox County, Oates won 6,270 votes out of a total of 6,401, while in Bullock County Kolb received only 292 votes to 2,309 for Oates.[49] Even more than Jones in 1892, Oates owed his victory to the Black Belt counties.

Kolb claimed that fraud in 1894 was worse than in 1892. Since the state had no law providing for contested elections, direct evidence of vote manipulation did not become a matter of record. In the November elections for Congress, however, several contests were made. A congressional committee, taking testimony in the disputed William F. Aldrich-Gaston A. Robbins election, discovered that in one Black Belt County the Democrats had cast votes in the name of Republican Negroes who had not registered and did not vote. Negroes who had been dead for years and others who had long since left the state were also voted, and hundreds of fictitious names were added to the poll list. The Democratic frauds of November made more plausible Kolb's claim that the August election was stolen from him.[50]

Political machinations in the Black Belt determined the outcome of the elections, but the coal mining counties presented their own peculiar voting patern. In 1892, 20,053 votes were cast in Jefferson, Bibb, and Walker counties in the gubernatorial election; in 1894 only 13,965 votes were cast. Oates suffered far more than did Kolb in this diminution of the vote. Oates polled 4,138 fewer votes in Jefferson than had Jones in 1892, while Kolb's total declined by only 682. Despite this disparity of loss, Oates won Jefferson County by the slim plurality of 22 votes. In the counties of Bibb and Walker, Kolb won in 1894 as he had in 1892. He had slightly reduced majorities from a greatly reduced total vote.[51] Although a few votes made no difference in the state-wide election, the results in Jefferson County demonstrated the effects of removing strikers from the state. Otherwise, Kolb would have carried the county. Ignoring the question of fraud, a charge not raised in these counties, it is clear that the miners were not able to muster the vote for Kolb that the circumstances indicated. In any event, no Kolb victory in the mineral counties could have offset the made to order vote of the Black Belt.

For a brief time it seemed that the disappointed followers of Kolb might resort to violence and revolution. Miners declaimed that "if Kolb is elected we ought to put him [in] if we have to take up arms to do it. . . ."[52] The belligerent mood soon passed and was replaced by the apathy and disillusionment of defeat. Daniel S. Troy, Montgomery lawyer and apostate Democrat, spoke for the Jeffersonians and the miners as he cried:

God help the people of Alabama, for they are in a condition of the lost soul, which in life neglected its opportunity, and as it wings its flight to Plutonian shores, cries out in anguish 'Lost! Lost! Forever lost'![53]

chapter **8**

"The Agony Is Over"

The coal miners' hope for a political solution to their economic battle was destroyed by the results of the election. That Kolb could have brought immediate relief seems doubtful. He would not have been inaugurated until December, but his election would have created an atmosphere of optimism for the miners. Once in office he undoubtedly would have pressed for legislation favorable to the miners.

Through four long months the strikers had maintained their cause. Now, in August, only the most dedicated or belligerent had heart to continue the battle. The vote had proved as ineffectual as economic pressure in bringing victory for labor. In the degrees and shadings of defeat there were gains that could be preserved, advances that could be maintained. Miner solidarity throughout the travail of settlement could save the union as a viable force for the future.

A week before the election there were already signs of

cleavage within the miners' union. Throughout the mining camps disheartened miners began to talk of settlement and an end to the strike. Such attitudes were denounced by the more dedicated who drew up lists of names to stigmatize their weaker brothers.[1] Taking cognizance of this threat to organization, the miners' executive committee distributed a circular to its local councils, noting that a number of miners had attempted "to effect a settlement of our present trouble without the aid or knowledge of said committee or the miners at large. . . ." Such individuals were "enemies and traitors to themselves, their friends, and their fellow miners of Alabama."[2]

More than pronunciamentos by the executive committee were needed to stay the tide of settlement. Earlier, Governor Jones had declared that troops would be kept in the mining district until the strike was ended. On August 6, he informed Lt. Erwin of his desire to remove the troops as soon as possible. Erwin was instructed to investigate the state of readiness of the armed citizen groups being organized in Birmingham by Joseph F. Johnston, Oates's opponent for the Democratic nomination earlier in the year. "It will be well," said the governor, "to let DeBardeleben and others know that we are thinking of taking the troops away so they can make preparations."[3]

The basis of the governor's optimism was soon made public. On August 7, the Tennessee Company offered a new proposition to its miners. As in the company's earlier offer of July 11, miners' wages were to be tied to the market price of iron. Whereas the July offer had promised a wage scale of 35 cents a ton, the new proposition offered a scale of 37½ cents.[4] In morning and afternoon sessions on the day of the election, August 8, the miners' executive committee deliberated the issues of the company offer. The vise of circumstance was closing on the harried members of the committee. On one hand they faced the growing dissatisfaction and defection of their membership —bound to increase under the new offer of the operators. Here was potent pressure to accept the operators' offer and end the strike. In contradistinction, the committee was restricted by the decisions reached by the miners' convention of July 13. They had been specifically ordered not to call another convention until the demand for 45 cents a ton had been met.[5] The committee could discuss lower offers, but in order to agree to a general settlement (encompassing the Tennessee and Sloss companies) a convention was necessary to ratify it. The executive committee was entertaining an offer from the Tennessee Company alone. It was considering a settlement that did not include the miners of the Sloss Company. At four o'clock on the afternoon of August 8, President Fournier announced that the Tennesse Company's offer had been rejected. Although he did not mention it, an important jurisdictional question was involved. Prior to the miners' convention of July 13, the executive committee had been empowered to negotiate with single companies, but it was not to call off the strike against either the Tennessee or Sloss companies until an agreement had been reached with both. Without alluding to these restrictions, Fournier simply said that "the reason for the rejection was that the proposition was not sufficient."[6] Although Fournier added that the "miners do not seem satisfied unless they get 45 cents," the committee made a counter offer to the Tennessee Company of 40 cents a ton.[7] According to Detective "E. W.," the "majority of miners here wanted to settle and were willing . . ." to accept the offer of 37½ cents.[8] The counter offer was rejected by the company, but negotiations continued.

On August 11, Governor Jones, convinced that the strike was nearing its end, informed Lt. Erwin, "I have determined to remove all the troops from Jefferson County. . . ." The governor's aids in Birmingham would be relieved and the Pinkerton detectives sent home.[9] There was solid foundation for the governor's actions. The miners' executive committee, unable to dissuade the Tennessee Company from its offer of 37½ cents, had submitted the offer to the miners of Pratt, Blocton, and Blue Creek.[10]

An estimated 1,000 miners in the Blocton area met to consider the company's offer on August 14. The Blocton miners had been the last to feel the full impact of the strike. Not until July 21 were they faced with eviction from company houses or threatened with outside labor importation.[11] Meeting now, they were addressed by "ex-superintendent Thomas,"[12] who informed them that the strike was lost. There was nothing left to do but go back to work and make the best of the situation.[13] With only three dissenting votes the Blocton miners voted to accept the Tennessee Company's offer and resume work.[14] At the Pratt Mines, the strikers voted in favor of acceptance by a five to one majority,[15] but there is no evidence of a meeting or a vote by the Blue Creek miners. In the light of subsequent developments, it seems likely that if a meeting was held, the offer was voted down.

With the approval of a majority of the Tennessee Company miners, the union executive committee met with the officers of the company on the night of August 15. A final discussion of the company's offer ensued, agreement was reached, and a contract was signed.[16] President Fournier issued orders raising the suspension against the Tennessee Company.

The basic provisions of the new contract were less favorable to the miners than DeBardeleben's original offer of July 11.[17] The Pratt Mines scale established a minimum price of 37½ cents per ton

when No. 1 foundry iron nets the Tennessee . . . Company $8.50 or less F.O.B. cars at the furnace, and for every advance of 50 cents in the net price received for iron, there shall be an increase of 2½ cents in the price of mining until the net price received for iron reaches $11 per ton, when the price of mining will be fifty cents a ton. Thereafter the price of mining shall advance 2½ cents for each one dollar advance in the net price received for iron.[18]

Other mines would be paid on the Pratt scale, except at Blocton where higher prices would be paid if the coal seam narrowed. All mines that had checkweighmen as of July 1893 could continue to use them, "at other mines coal to be paid for by the car, as was the case at that time."[19] In accordance with the demands of the miners, powder would be reduced to $1.60 a keg, and house rents would be lowered by 10 per cent. As a temporary concession the company agreed that "for three months only the Tennessee . . . Company will pay its miners . . . twice a month."[20] No discrimination was to be shown in the re-employment of strikers, "except those guilty of crime, who will not be employed."[21]

The miners thus accepted a lower wage scale than they had been willing to concede before the strike was called, and lower than the miners' conventions had demanded as the basis for a settlement. In neither case, however, had the miners asked for an escalator clause. No gains had been made on the issue of checkweighmen, although the men won the question on the price of supplies and housing. On balance, the new contract did not bear the hallmarks of total defeat. The miners had not been forced to accept a peace at any price.

The *Labor Advocate* headlined the settlement, "The Agony is Over."[22] The *Age-Herald* characterized the settlement as "just, fair, and equitable to all parties concerned," and hoped "for a season of order, peace, prosperity, and plenty!"[23] The Tuscaloosa *Gazette* was equally enthusiastic. The settlement "is a cause of rejoicing to the whole state. . . . Birmingham will brighten and the rest of the country will profit proportionately."[24]

Amid the jubilation and optimism there remained elements

of unhappiness and anger. Reporting the settlement, the *Labor Advocate* had brightly prophesied that "the Sloss and other miners will no doubt follow the good example."[25] Such statements were galling to the Sloss strikers. They had joined the strike when the miners of the Tennessee Company had failed to gain their demands. When the Walker County miners had returned to work, the Sloss miners had staunchly supported the cause. It had been agreed that no settlement would be made without the consent of both companies. Now the Sloss strikers stood alone. The last ounce of their negotiating power was nullified by the actions of the executive committee. They had no choice but to return to work. But if the strikers of Sloss were forgotten by their executive committee, their predicament did not go unnoticed by the miners of Blue Creek. Under the leadership of William Mailley a mass meeting of the Blue Creek miners was held at Adger on August 15. In a sharp attack on the executive committee, the meeting adopted resolutions protesting the settlement. The executive committee had signed a contract without authorization by "the miners in general" as had been earlier agreed. It had made a settlement not based on propositions approved by the general membership. And further:

> By calling the strike off at the . . . Tennessee Company's mines, the striking miners at the mines of the Sloss Iron and Steel Company have been left to fight their battle out alone. When Walker returned to work, it was agreed upon in convention that the Sloss . . . and the Tennessee . . . miners stay out together until both were settled. There was to be no agreement with either company until both settled.[26]

Except in the moral sphere the support of the Blue Creek miners was of little avail to the deserted strikers at Sloss. Those that the company was willing to rehire went back to work, but there was no guarantee of re-employment.[27] Many strikers believed their fellow miners had given in too easily and for them the strike ended on the sour note of betrayal and desertion.

Other principals in the four month drama fared little better. Despite the arrest of over one hundred miners for the murders at the Pratt Mines, only fouteen were ever brought to trial. W. J. Kelso, the supposed leader in the Massacre, was convicted of manslaughter and sentenced to one year at hard labor in the mines, although some thought Kelso lent a touch of professionalism to amateur convict labor.[28] Difficulties also stalked the career of Henry F. DeBardeleben. With the strike ended, DeBardeleben thought boom and prosperity were on the horizon. In a direct onslaught on Wall Street, he attempted to gain majority control of the Tennessee Company, but his speculation ended in disaster. He lost his stock in the company, and late in 1894 resigned from his position as vice-president.[29] Governor Jones rode out the storm with little difficulty. At the end of his term he returned to the practice of law, assured of a position with the Louisville & Nashville "to continue during 'good behavior.' "[30]

In the words of Governor Jones, the strike of 1894 was the "most formidable and threatening commotion in the history of this State in times of peace."[31] The United Mine Workers of Alabama had been organized in a time of depression and unemployment. It had conducted a strike of four months' duration in the face of overwhelming opposition by the operators. The union had also to contend with public opinion that grew increasingly hostile and a state government that had never before faced problems between management and labor on such a massive scale. For the young union to have survived the struggle was a victory. And it did survive, though rebuilding was slow. A state convention was held in October 1894. The only miner from the Tennessee Company elected to office was William Mailley, the leader of the Adger protest against the August settlement.[32]

Throughout the 1894 strike, the parties to the issue acted out their classic roles from the script of industrial warfare. A prevailing concept in the 1800's was that labor, like railroad cars and hoisting machinery, had no part in determining wages, rents, and charges. When labor revolted, whether its claims were legitimate or not, there was an inevitable resistance on the part of management.

The cost to the state for Governor Jones's decision to have the state militia present in the Birmingham area was at least $48,-514.[33] To the governor it was not too high a price to pay to give "to the world assurance that the blessings of peace and enlightened government are nowhere more highly prized, or better secured against domination of mobs, than in our midst."[34] Governor Jones played a pivotal role throughout the strike. He admitted the right of the miners to strike and denied the state's authority to decide the economic issues. But the miners charged that he did not limit himself to the prevention of violence. He actively intervened, they claimed, to persuade the operators to use blackleg labor, promising them protection from the violence that his advice engendered. The miners exaggerated Jones's hostility to their cause, but he was the product of an agrarian tradition and unfamiliar with labor's aspirations. He believed in the right to strike, but he also believed in the freedom of contract. As the governor told the state legislature, he had upheld "the sacred right of the workingman to determine for himself when, for whom, and at what price he will labor. . . ."[35] The miners, as union men, operated from a far different premise, but in 1894 they were unable to convince the public that they had a legitimate case.

To treat Alabama populism as a simple and naïve farmers' movement is to deny its diversity and overlook its complexity. The shibboleth of the agrarian South cannot obscure the non-agrarian genesis of reform in the state. Elements of labor made the transition from economic protest to political action prior to the political revolt of the farmers. As one historian has recently written, "Farmers felt at one with workers, not through an ideology of producer values but a conviction that both groups had been reduced to the same economic position."[36] Both groups stirred in protest against the rulers of the New South, against an economic and political structure of considerable inequity. The stigma of change fell on the embattled agrarians and their union allies as they sought to control government in their own interest. In a final sense, Kolb and Fournier were no more radical than Jones and DeBardeleben. Each desired to use the state positively to promote a particular set of principles and ideals.

There were few rewards for the cause of reform. The farmer-labor attempt to unseat the Bourbons ended in failure. Honesty at the ballot box was restored at the price of excluding the Negro from political affairs. For the miners the era of protest was the painful beginning of years of repetitive struggle. Yet amid the residue of defeat it was possible to philosophize that even lost causes add their small but essential element to the complex equation of change.

Notes

CHAPTER 1

1. A major study of the Alabama strike has never been made. C. Vann Woodward in his *Origins of the New South* (Baton Rouge, 1951), 266-67 gives a brief resumé to illustrate the South's involvement in industrial violence and political reform. A more detailed treatment can be found in Holman Head, "The Development of the Labor Movement in Alabama Prior to 1900" (Master's thesis, Alabama, 1955), 82-106. Martha C. Mitchell, "Birmingham: Biography of a City of the New South" (unpubl. diss., Chicago, 1946), 128-31, gives a brief account of it.

2. Geographic and geologic information on the coal fields may be found in Saffold Berney, *Handbook of Alabama* (Birmingham, 1892), 403-08, 471-74; A. M. Gibson, *Geological Survey of Alabama; Report Upon the Coosa Coal Field* (Montgomery, 1895); Joseph Squire, *Geological Survey of Alabama; Report on the Cahaba Coal Field* (Montgomery, 1890); and Ethel Armes, *The Story of Coal and Iron in Alabama* (Birmingham, 1910), *passim*.

3. A brief treatment of this early period is in George M. Cruickshank, *A History of Birmingham and its Environs*, 2 vols. (New York,

1920), I, 18-21. More detailed is the romanticized but valuable work by Armes, chaps. II-VI.

4. Squire, 18; Virginia Knapp, "William Phineas Brown, Business Man and Pioneer Mine Operator of Alabama," Pt. 1, *Alabama Review,* III (April, 1950), 108-22; Pt. 2 (July, 1950), 193-99.

5. Squire, 18. See the more detailed account by Squire quoted in Armes, 152-56.

6. Frank E. Vandiver, "The Shelby Iron Company in the Civil War: A Study of a Confederate Industry," Pt. 3, *Alabama Review,* I (July, 1948), 216-17; Joseph H. Woodward, "Alabama Iron Manufacturing, 1860-1865," *ibid.,* VII (July, 1954), 199-207.

7. Frank E. Vandiver, "Joseph Gorgas and the Brierfield Iron Works," *Alabama Review,* III (January, 1950), 7.

8. *Ibid.,* 6-21.

9. Armes, 238.

10. Quoted in *ibid.,* 252.

11. Cruickshank, II, 5-7, 367-70; John Leeds Kerr, *The Louisville & Nashville; An Outline History* (New York, 1933), 36-39.

12. Anne Kendrick Walker, *Life and Achievements of Alfred Montgomery Shook* (Birmingham, 1952), 75-88; Arthur V. Wiebel, *Biography of a Business* (Birmingham, 1960), *passim.*

13. See Virginia Pounds Bacon and Jane Porter Nabers, "The Origin of Certain Place Names in Jefferson County, Alabama," *Alabama Review,* V (July, 1952), 177-202; "James Bowron Scrapbook," 2 vols., Birmingham Public Library, Birmingham, Ala.; Wiebel, *passim.*

14. *Mineral Resources of the United States, 1893* (Washington, 1894), 240-45.

15. Montgomery *Advertiser,* Jan. 16, 1869, quoting Memphis *Ledger.*

16. Montgomery *Advertiser,* Apr. 1, 1871, quoting Elyton *Sun.*

17. *Ninth Census,* 1870, Population, I, 11; *ibid.,* 1880, 340; *ibid.,* 1890, 402.

18. Berney, 345.

19. John R. Harnady, *The Book of Birmingham* (New York, 1921), 1.

20. Reuben F. Kolb to R. H. Edmonds, Mar. 29, 1888, Department of Agriculture Letter Book, No. 197, Alabama Department of Archives and History, Montgomery.

21. Head, 83; *Report of Special Committee to Investigate Mining Industries in the State, 1897,* 7.

22. Head, 83.

23. Tuscaloosa *Gazette,* Apr. 17, 1879.

24. Birmingham *Sunday Chronicle,* Aug. 23, 1885.

25. *Ibid.*

26. Aug. 30, 1885.

27. Head, 83.

28. On the difficulties encountered by Negro labor, see Sterling D. Spero and Abram L. Harris, *The Black Worker; The Negro and the Labor Movement* (New York, 1931), and Herbert R. Northrup, *Organized Labor and the Negro* (New York, 1944).

29. *Annual Report of the Treasurer of the State of Alabama, For the Fiscal Year Ending September 30, 1894* (Montgomery, 1894), 23; *The Report of the Board of Health of the State of Alabama, For the Year 1895* (Montgomery, 1896), 27-35, 51. The origins and development of the convict lease system are clearly described in Allen J. Going, *Bourbon Democracy in Alabama, 1874-1890* (University, Alabama, 1951), 176-79. See also Fannie Ella Sapp, "The Convict Lease System in Alabama, 1846-1895" (Master's thesis, Peabody College, 1931), *passim.*

30. *First Biennial Report of the Board of Inspectors of Convicts to the Governor, From September 1, 1894 to August 31, 1896* (Montgomery, 1896), statistical exhibits.

31. George Sinclair Mitchell, "Labor Disputes and Organization," in *Culture in the South,* ed. W. T. Couch (Chapel Hill, 1934), 629-45.

32. Head, 84.

33. Birmingham *Weekly Independent,* Apr. 22, 1880.

34. Birmingham *Observer,* Apr. 22, 1880.

35. Birmingham *Weekly Independent,* July 17, 1880.

36. Head, 85-86.

37. *Ibid.,* 85. The strike is listed in *Report of the Secretary of the Interior,* . . . (Washington, 1887), V, 36-37, as not ordered by a labor organization.

38. *Report of the Secretary of the Interior,* V, 36-39. The strike is listed by the Commissioner of Labor as not ordered by a labor organization, although its duration would argue for more cohesion than the miners generally showed. The government listed wages on a per day basis, although a per ton scale was the standard in mining.

39. *Ibid.,* V, 36-37.

40. *Ibid.,* V, 36-39.

41. *Ibid.*

42. Birmingham *Sunday Chronicle*, Sept. 6, 1885.

43. Birmingham *Evening Chronicle*, July 19, 1885.

44. *Ibid.*

45. *Ibid.*

46. Aug. 2, 1885. For the later activities of the League, see *ibid.*, Aug. 30, 1885; Sept. 6, 1885; Sept. 12, 1885.

47. Head, 87.

48. *Report of the Secretary of the Interior*, II, 34-35.

49. Head, 86-87.

50. *Ibid.*

51. Birmingham *Alamaba News Digest*, Jan. 25, 1940; Head, 87-88.

52. *Ibid.*, 88-89; *Report of the Secretary of the Interior*, II, 34-35.

53. *Ibid.*, II, 34-37.

CHAPTER 2

1. Head, 90.

2. Birmington *Labor Advocate* (hereafter *Labor Advocate*), May 10, 1890.

3. *Ibid.*

4. *Ibid.*, July 4, 1890.

5. *Ibid.*

6. *Report of the Secretary of the Interior*, V, 38-41.

7. *Labor Advocate*, Nov. 8, 1890.

8. *Ibid.*, Jan. 10, 1891.

9. *Mineral Resources of the United States*, 241.

10. *Labor Advocate*, Dec. 6, 13, 1890; Jan. 24, 1891.

11. *Ibid.*, Dec. 20, 1890; Jan. 2, 1891.

12. *Ibid.*, Jan. 24, 1891.

13. *Ibid.*, Jan. 21, 1891.

14. *Ibid.*, Feb. 21, 1891.

15. This account of the organization of the United Mine Workers in Alabama and their strike of 1890-1891 is at variance with the findings of Head in his "Labor Movement in Alabama," 90-92. Head concludes that "there apparently was some form of affiliation at first, but District 20 of the United Mine Workers of America was not actively established in Alabama until 1898." There is conclusive evidence that the United Mine Workers of America was actively established in Ala-

bama from May 1890 to at least March 1891. The Miners' Trades Council was not deliberating the question of a state federation, but whether to join the UMW of America. Executive board members of the national UMW were present in Alabama during the wage talks at Pratt and during the strike itself. The Birmingham Trades Council received a letter during the strike asking for moral support, specifically identified as coming from the "local branch of the United Mine Workers of America." See *Labor Advocate,* Dec. 20, 1890. Short-lived it certainly was, but the United Mine Workers of America was actively established in Alabama in 1890.

16. *Mineral Resources of the United States,* 241.

17. *Labor Advocate,* Mar. 26, 1892.

18. Florence Hawkins Wood Moss, *Building Birmingham and Jefferson County* (Birmingham, 1947), 130.

19. *Birmingham Evening Chronicle,* Apr. 21, 30, 1886. See also *Jefferson County and Birmingham: Historical and Biographical, 1887* (Birmingham, 1887), 201.

20. Martha C. Mitchell, "Birmingham," 192. See also *Labor Advocate,* Jan. 17, 1890.

21. All the printed sources attribute the founding and publication of the *Labor Advocate* to J. H. F. Mosley. Martha C. Mitchell, 192, refers to him as George Mosley; this identification of Mosley as the founder seems to rest on Cruickshank, I, 106. Dennis speaks of himself as the editor and publisher of the paper, and it seems probable that he was the founder.

22. *Labor Advocate* (no date. January, 1890?).

23. *Ibid.,* Jan. 17, 1890.

24. *Ibid.,* Jan. 6, 1894.

25. For comment on the relationship of the Bourbons to business see Going, 113, 116-17.

26. There was an active Greenback Party in Alabama in the 1880's, and it seems to have won some support for reform principles. For information on the Agricultural Wheel in Alabama see William W. Rogers, "Agrarianism in Alabama, 1865-1896" (Unpubl. diss., North Carolina, 1959), 216-34.

27. Moulton *Advertiser,* Aug. 8, 25, 1887; Hartsell *Alabama Enquirer,* Dec. 1, 1887.

28. Moulton *Advertiser,* Sept. 17, 1887. See also Montgomery *Advertiser,* Sept. 27, 1887; Birmingham *Weekly Iron Age,* Sept. 22, 1887.

29. Montgomery *Advertiser,* Mar. 23, 1888.

30. *Ibid.,* Mar. 24, 1888.

31. Moulton *Advertiser,* Mar. 17, 1887.

32. Rogers, "Agrarianism," 231.

33. For the growth of the Alliance up to 1890 see William Warren Rogers, "The Farmers' Alliance in Alabama," *Alabama Review,* XV (January, 1962), 5-18.

34. Rogers, "Agrarianism," 247.

35. Quoted in Montgomery *Advertiser,* Jan. 8, 1890.

36. Rogers, "Agrarianism," 291-93.

37. *Ibid.,* 318-19.

38. *Ibid.,* 337-40. The reappointment would have been for an interim period pending the election of a commissioner.

39. See John Harkins to Governor Jones, Mar. 8, 1891; Harkins and Lynch to Jones, Mar. 16, 1891, Thomas G. Jones Papers, Alabama Department of Archives and History, Montgomery (hereafter Jones Papers).

40. Dennis Canning to Jones, Mar. 10, 1891, in *ibid.* On this same issue see J. A. Montgomery to Jones, Mar. 14, 1891, and Sterling S. Lanier to Jones, Mar. 12, 1891, in *ibid.*

41. Rogers, "Agrarianism," 342-43.

42. Seale *Russell Register,* Jan. 2, 1892.

43. L. W. Johns to Jones, Dec. 23, 1891, Jones Papers. See also J. W. Bush to Jones, Dec. 21, 1891, in *ibid.,* who referred to the mines at Blue Creek and Pratt as "strong holds of yours."

44. See John C. Carmichael to Jones, Dec. 24, 1891, in *ibid.,* for evidence on campaign expenditures in Jefferson County.

45. Grove Hill *Clarke County Democrat,* Apr. 21, 1892.

46. *Ibid.*

47. See the Union Springs *Herald,* Apr. 27, 1892; Butler *Choctaw Advocate,* Apr. 27, 1892, quoting the Selma *Mirror.*

48. R. F. Kolb to T. A. Street, Apr. 22, 1892, Street Papers, University of Alabama Library.

49. Butler *Choctaw Advocate,* May 11, 1892, quoting Columbus *Sun.*

50. Birmingham *Daily News,* June 11, 1892; Montgomery *Advertiser,* June 9, 1892; Eufaula *Times and News,* June 16, 1892.

51. Rogers, "Agrarianism," 368.

52. For the complete text of the platform see Montgomery *Advertiser,* June 10, 1892.

53. Chappell Cory to Jones, Aug. 14, 1892, Jones Papers. For a de-

tailed account of the campaign and analysis of the election returns see Rogers, "Agrarianism," chap. XIV.

54. H. F. DeBardeleben to Jones, Jan. 1, 1892, Jones Papers.

55. M. H. Smith to Jones, Feb. 16, 1893, in *ibid.*

56. Randolph Peyton to Jones, Aug. 19, 1892, in *ibid.*

57. Bessemer *Journal,* Nov. 24, 1892. For Jones' views on the convict question see *Message of Hon. Thos. G. Jones, Governor of Alabama,* 1892 (Montgomery, 1892), 15-16.

58. *Labor Advocate,* Feb. 4, 1893.

59. *Ibid.*

60. *Ibid.,* Mar. 10, 1894.

61. *Ibid.*

62. Birmingham *Age-Herald* (hereafter *Age-Herald*), Mar. 11, 1894. See also Mobile *Daily News,* Mar. 22, 1894.

63. *Mineral Resources of the United States,* 240.

64. *Origins of the New South,* 264n.

65. *Labor Advocate,* June 22, 1893.

66. *Mineral Resources of the United States,* 240.

67. Armes, 426-27.

68. *Labor Advocate,* June 22, 1893; *Report of the Secretary of the Interior,* V, 38-41.

69. Bessemer *Journal,* June 29, 1893.

70. Milton H. Smith to Jones, June 24, 1893, Jones Papers; *Age-Herald,* July 1, 1893.

71. *Labor Advocate,* Feb. 25 and Oct. 14, 1893; *Age-Herald,* Oct. 5, 1893. For details and correspondence on the miners' strike of 1893 and the use of troops at New Decatur see *Biennial Report of the Adjutant General of Alabama to Thomas G. Jones,* 1894 (Montgomery, 1894), 41-48.

72. *Labor Advocate,* June 29, 1893.

73. July 2, 1893. The *Age-Herald's* account of the meeting is in great detail. See also *Labor Advocate,* July 6, 1893.

74. *Ibid.,* July 27, 1893.

75. *Ibid.,* Oct. 7, 1893. See also *Age-Herald,* Oct. 5, 1893.

76. See the letter from "Grey Goose" in the *Labor Advocate,* Oct. 7, 1893.

77. On the organization of the union see *Labor Advocate,* Oct. 21, 1893; Head, 94-95.

78. *Labor Advocate,* Nov. 4, 1893.

79. *Ibid.,* Nov. 18, 1893.

80. *Ibid.,* Nov. 11, 1893.
81. *Ibid.,* Nov. 11, Oct. 28, 1893.
82. Head, 95.
83. *Labor Advocate,* Nov. 11, 1893.
84. *Ibid.,* Oct. 21, Dec. 9, 1893.
85. *Ibid.,* Nov. 18, 1893.
86. *Ibid.,* Dec. 30, 1893.
87. *Ibid.,* Jan. 6, 20, 1894.
88. *Ibid.,* Jan. 20, 1894.
89. *Ibid.,* Mar. 24, 1894.
90. *Ibid.,* Jan. 20, 1894.
91. *Ibid.,* Mar. 10, 17, 1894.
92. *Ibid.,* Mar. 17, 1894.
93. *Ibid.,* Mar. 10, 1894.
94. *Ibid.,* Mar. 17, 1894.
95. *Ibid.,* Jan. 27, 1894.
96. *Ibid.*
97. *Ibid.,* Jan. 20, 1894.
98. *Ibid.,* Jan. 20, 27, 1894.
99. *Ibid.,* Feb. 10, 1894.
100. *Ibid.*
101. *Ibid.,* Mar. 17, 24, 1894.
102. *Ibid.,* Mar. 30, 1894.
103. *Ibid.*
104. *Ibid.,* Mar. 17, 1894.
105. *Ibid.,* Feb. 10, 1894.
106. *Ibid.,* Mar. 30, 1894. See also the interesting letter from "Laborer" in the Bessemer *Journal,* Mar. 29, 1894.
107. *Labor Advocate,* June 9, 1894.

CHAPTER 3

1. *Labor Advocate,* Apr. 7, 1894.
2. *Ibid.*
3. *Ibid.* In reviewing the negotiations, the union executive committee later reported that the miners had offered a 5.0 per cent wage reduction. Computations from reported per ton wage bases show that the offer was for 10 per cent reductions as originally reported. See *ibid.,* Apr. 21, 1894. For miner dissatisfaction with the medical system,

emphasizing a later period, see Bruce Crawford, "The Coal Miner," in *Culture in the South*, 365.

4. *Labor Advocate*, Apr. 7, 1894.

5. *Ibid*. See the reply of the state convict manager, Samuel Will John, in *ibid.*, Apr. 14, 1894.

6. This follows the account given by "Pendragon" in *ibid*.

7. Bessemer *Weekly*, Apr. 7, 1894.

8. "Pendragon" in the *Labor Advocate*, Apr. 14, 1894.

9. *Ibid*.

10. Statement of the union executive committee in *ibid.*, Apr. 21, 1894.

11. Bessemer *Weekly*, Apr. 14, 1894; *Labor Advocate*, Apr. 21, 1894.

12. Chris Evans, *History of the United Mine Workers of America*, 2 vols. (n. p., 1920), II, 320.

13. *Ibid.*, II, 328-31. See also New York *Times*, Apr. 15, 16, 17, 19, 23, 1894.

14. *Labor Advocate*, Apr. 21, 1894.

15. Bessemer *Weekly*, Apr. 14, 1894, quoting the *Age-Herald*.

16. *Ibid*.

17. Apr. 21, 1894.

18. Bessemer *Weekly*, Apr. 14, 1894, quoting the *Age-Herald*.

19. *Ibid*.

20. *Ibid*.

21. Apr. 7, 1894.

22. Apr. 15, 1894.

23. Apr. 14, 1894.

24. Apr. 19, 1894.

25. *Age-Herald*, Apr. 22, 1894.

26. *Ibid.*, Apr. 24, 1894; Mobile *Daily News*, Apr. 22, 1894.

27. *Age-Herald*, Apr. 24, 1894.

28. *Ibid*.

29. *Ibid*.

30. *Age-Herald*, Apr. 22, 1894.

31. *Labor Advocate*, Apr. 21, 1894.

32. *Ibid*.

33. *Ibid*.

34. *Age-Herald*, Apr. 15, 1894.

35. *Labor Advocate*, Apr. 21, 1894, quoting the *Age-Herald*.

36. Mobile *Daily News*, Apr. 22, 1894; *Labor Advocate*, May 5, 1894.

37. May 7, 1894.

38. *Labor Advocate,* May 5, 1894.

39. *Ibid.,* Apr. 21, 1894.

40. April 23, 1894.

41. *Report of the Adjutant General,* 49.

42. Message of Governor Jones to the Legislature, Nov. 14, 1894, *Journal of the House of Representatives of the State of Alabama, Session of 1894-1895* (Montgomery, 1895), 37; Mobile *Daily News,* Apr. 23, 1894; *Report of the Adjutant General,* 49.

43. Message to the Legislature, 1894, 37.

44. *Ibid.; Age-Herold,* Apr. 24, 1894.

45. *Ibid.*

46. Mobile *Daily News,* Apr. 23, 1894; *Labor Advocate,* Apr. 28, 1894.

47. Apr. 23, 1894.

48. *Age-Herald,* Apr. 24, 1894.

49. *Ibid.*

50. *Ibid.,* Apr. 28, 1894.

51. Message to the Legislature, 1894, 37.

52. Bessemer *Weekly,* Apr. 28, 1894.

53. *Ibid.*

54. *Ibid.,* May 5, 1894.

55. Bessemer *Journal,* Apr. 26, 1894.

56. *Ibid.*

57. *Labor Advocate,* Apr. 28, 1894.

58. Mobile *Daily News,* May 7, 1894.

59. May 5, 1894.

60. *Ibid.*

61. *Ibid.*

62. *Ibid.*

63. *Ibid.*

64. *Ibid.*

CHAPTER 4

1. *Age-Herald,* May 8, 1894. See also *Labor Advocate,* May 12, 1894. Early reports of the attack gave the number involved as from 100 to 500. See the telegram, J. T. Morgan to Governor Jones, May 7, 1894, *Report of the Adjutant General,* 50

2. *Age-Herald,* May 8, 1894.

3. Message to the Legislature, 1894, 38. See the telegrams, Morgan to Jones, May 7, 1894; G. H. Guttery to Jones, May 7, 1894; Jones to Guttery, May 7, 1894; Jones to Clark, May 7, 1894; Morrow to Jones, May 7, 1894, all in *Report of the Adjutant General,* 50-52.

4. May 10, 1894.

5. May 12, 1894.

6. *Ibid.*

7. *Ibid.*

8. Message to the Legislature, 1894, 37.

9. *Age-Herald,* May 8, 1894.

10. Governor Jones to Lt. James B. Erwin, Adjutant Generals Records, Correspondence, Alabama Department of Archives and History, Montgomery.

11. *Report of the Adjutant General,* 52

12. *Labor Advocate,* May 19, 1894. See also *ibid.,* May 12, 1894.

13. Mobile *Daily News,* May 11, 1894; *Age-Herald,* May 10, 1894.

14. Message to the Legislature, 1894, 37.

15. See T. N. Vallens to Jones, Sept. 9, 1891; Pinkerton's National Detective Agency to Jones, Oct. 25, 31, Nov. 2, 12, 1893; Vallens to Jones, Nov. 4, 1893; Vallens to Jones, Apr. 2, 27, 1894, all in Jones Papers.

16. Erwin to Jones, May 17, 1894, Jones Papers. The usual procedure was for Lt. Erwin to summarize the agents' report in a letter or telegram to the governor. Sometimes the agents wrote or wired the governor directly, and in addition, the detective agency also sent summaries of the reports to Jones.

17. Mobile *Daily News,* May 11, 1894.

18. *Ibid.* For violence and rumors of violence see the telegrams: Morrow to Jones, May 8, 1894; Rollins to Jones, May 8, 1894; Rodgers to Jones, May 10, 1894; Morrow to Jones, May 10, 1894, all in *Report of the Adjutant General,* 52-53.

19. Erwin to Jones, May 17, 1894, Jones Papers. Erwin does not mention this meeting in his public report.

20. *Labor Advocate,* May 12, 1894.

21. *Age-Herald,* May 10, 1894.

22. May 12, 1894.

23. Bessemer *Weekly,* May 19, 1894; *Labor Advocate,* May 19, 1894.

24. See Erwin to Jones, May 15, 1894, Jones Papers.

25. Bessemer *Weekly,* May 26, 1894.

26. Erwin to Jones, May 17, 1894, Jones Papers.

27. *Labor Advocate,* May 19, 1894.

28. *Age-Herald,* May 22, 1894; Erwin to Jones, May 15, 1894, Jones Papers.

29. May 26, 1894.

30. See *Report of the Adjutant General,* 54.

31. Erwin to Jones, May 15, 1894, Jones Papers.

32. *Labor Advocate,* May 19, 26, 1894.

33. *Ibid.,* May 19, 1894.

34. *Ibid.,* May 12, 19, 1894.

35. *Ibid.,* May 19, 1894.

36. *Age-Herald,* May 10, 1894.

37. *Ibid.*

38. May 12, 1894.

39. See the vivid account of the evictions at Adger by the staunch unionist William Mailley in *ibid.,* May 26, 1894. See also *Age-Herald,* May 10, 1894.

40. *Labor Advocate,* May 12, 26, 1894.

41. Vallens to Jones, May 19, 1894, Jones Papers.

42. Erwin to Jones, May 22, 1894, *ibid.*

43. Erwin to Jones, May 17, 1894, *ibid.*

44. *Age-Herald,* May 22, 1894; Jacksonville *Republican,* May 26, 1894.

45. *Age-Herald,* May 22, 1894.

46. *Ibid.,* May 25, 1894.

47. Message to the Legislature, 1894, 38.

48. See the telegrams, Vallens to Jones, May, 1894, Jones Papers; Rollins to Jones, May 8, 1894; Rodgers to Jones, May 10, 1894, all in *Report of the Adjutant General,* 52-53.

49. Vallens to Jones, May 21, 1894, Jones Papers.

50. Erwin to Jones, May 22, 1894, *ibid.*

51. *Ibid.*

52. *Ibid.*

53. *Ibid.*

54. *Ibid.*

55. See McCormack to Erwin, May 24, Adjutant Generals Records, Correspondence.

56. See *Report of the Adjutant General,* 54.

57. Erwin to Jones, May 24, 1894, *ibid.*

58. *Age-Herald,* May 26, 1894. On Sheriff Morrow see *Historical*

Collections of Birmingham, Jefferson County and Alabama; Collected, Arranged and Edited by Hill Ferguson, Vol. 48, *Sheriffs of Jefferson County, 1819-1958,* Birmingham Public Library, Birmingham.

59. *Age-Herald,* May 26, 1894; see also Message to the Legislature, 1894, 44.

60. *Age-Herald,* May 26, 1894.

61. *Ibid.*

62. *Ibid.*

63. *Ibid.,* May 25, 1894.

64. May 30, 1894.

65. May 31, 1894.

CHAPTER 5

1. Vallens to Jones, May 25, 1894, Jones Papers.

2. Mobile *Daily News,* May 28, 1894; *Age-Herald,* May 29, 1894.

3. Vallens to Jones, May 26, 1894, Jones Papers. See also *Age-Herald,* May 29, 1894.

4. Vallens to Jones, May 26, 1894, Jones Papers.

5. Vallens to Jones, May 25, 1894, *ibid.*

6. *Ibid.*

7. Mobile *Daily News,* May 28, 1894; *Age-Herald,* May 29, 1894.

8. See Vallens to Jones, May 25, 1894, Jones Papers.

9. Vallens to Jones, May 28, 1894, *ibid.*

10. *Age-Herald,* May 31, 1894.

11. June 2, 1894.

12. *Labor Advocate,* June 16, 1894.

13. *Age-Herald,* June 7, 1894. See also *ibid.,* June 9, 1894; Vallens to Jones, June 4, 1894; J. H. F. to Jones, June 5, 1894, both in the Jones Papers.

14. Vallens to Jones, June 9, 1894, *ibid.*

15. *Ibid.*

16. *Age-Herald,* June 12, 1894; *Labor Advocate,* June 16, 1894.

17. M.A.M. in *ibid.,* June 9, 1894.

18. *Age-Herald,* May 31, June 3, 8, 1894.

19. *Ibid.,* June 3, 6, 8, 1894.

20. *Ibid.,* May 29, 1894.

21. *Ibid.*

22. See the complete report in *Labor Advocate,* June 9, 1894.

23. J.H.F. to Jones, June 9, 1894, Jones Papers.

24. *Labor Advocate,* June 16, 1894.

25. An unidentified miner from Brookside in *ibid.,* June 9, 1894.

26. *Report of the Adjutant General,* 55.

27. May 26, 1894. See also Tuscaloosa *Gazette,* May 31, 1894, for the activities of the Warrior Guards.

28. Erwin to Jones, n.d., Jones Papers.

29. *Age-Herald,* June 3, 1894.

30. Hayneville *Citizen-Examiner,* June 7, 1894.

31. Mobile *Daily News,* June 6, 1894.

32. *Ibid.*

33. Tuscaloosa *Gazette,* June 7, 1894.

34. *Ibid.*

35. Erwin stated that ones heard of the trouble at 10:00 P.M., *Report of the Adjutant General,* 55.

36. *Ibid.,* 56.

37. This account of the Blue Creek affair is based on the *Age-Herald,* June 8, 9, 1894; Mobile *Daily News,* June 8, 1894; *Labor Advocate,* June 16, 1894; Message to the Legislature, 1894, 39.

38. *Ibid.,* 39.

39. *Age-Herald,* June 9, 1894.

40. *Labor Advocate,* June 16, 1894.

41. Message to the Legislature, 1894, 39; *Age-Herald,* June 12, 1894; *Report of the Adjutant General,* 56.

42. June 30, 1894.

43. *Ibid.*

44. *Age-Herald,* June 15, 1894.

45. June 2, 1894.

46. *Labor Advocate,* June 9, 1894.

47. *Age-Herald,* June 12, 1894.

48. Vallens to Jones, June 13, 1894, Jones Papers.

49. *Age-Herald,* June 13, 1894.

50. *Ibid.,* June 15, 1894; Mobile *Daily News,* June 17, 1894.

51. *Age-Herald,* June 19, 1894.

52. *Ibid.,* June 15, 1894. See also *Labor Advocate,* June 16, 23, 1894.

53. See *Age-Herald,* June 16, 21, 22, 1894; Mobile *Daily News,* June 21, 1894; *Labor Advocate,* June 23, 30, 1894.

54. *Age-Herald,* June 5, 1894.

55. *Ibid.,* June 12, 1894.

56. *Ibid.,* June 10, 14, 1894; *Labor Advocate,* June 16, 1894.

57. *Age-Herald,* June 14, 1894.

58. *Labor Advocate,* June 16, 1894.

59. *Ibid.*

60. June 16, 1894.

61. June 23, 1894.

62. June 6, 1894.

63. June 23, 1894.

64. *Labor Advocate.* Several of such poems, read consecutively to the operators, might well have forced a settlement in record time!

65. These are the attendance figures given by the *Age-Herald,* June 19, 1894. Detective Vallens estimated attendance at between 1,200 and 1,500, while the *Labor Advocate* claimed that 4,000 miners were present. See Vallens to Jones, June 18, 1894, Jones Papers; *Labor Advocate,* June 23, 1894.

66. *Age-Herald,* June 19, 1894.

67. *Labor Advocate,* June 30, 1894.

68. *Age-Herald,* June 19, 1894. Samuel M. Adams was the militant president of the Farmers' Alliance of Alabama.

69. *Labor Advocate,* June 30, 1894.

70. Vallens to Jones, June 18, 1894, Jones Papers.

71. Bessemer *Weekly,* June 23, 1894; *Labor Advocate,* June 23, 1894.

72. Vallens to Jones, June 20, 1894, Jones Papers.

73. *Ibid.* See also Bessemer *Weekly,* June 23, 1894; *Labor Advocate,* June 23, 1894.

74. *Ibid.*

75. Smith to Aldrich, June 26, 1894, *Age-Herald,* June 28, 1894.

76. Aldrich to Smith, June 27, 1894, *Age-Herald,* June 28, 1894.

77. *Age-Herald,* June 28, 1894.

78. *Ibid.* See also Bessemer *Weekly,* June 30, 1894; *Labor Advocate,* June 30, 1894.

79. Message to the Legislature, 1894, 40.

80. *Age-Herald,* June 30, 1894; Message to the Legislature, 1894, 40; *Report of the Adjutant General,* 56.

CHAPTER 6

1. *Labor Advocate,* July 21, 1894, quoting *United Mine Workers Journal.*

2. *Age-Herald,* July 3, 1894.

3. *Ibid.*

4. *Ibid.,* July 4, 1894.

5. *Ibid.,* July 6, 1894.

6. *Labor Advocate,* July 7, 1894.

7. See Chapter 5.

8. *Labor Advocate,* June 30, 1894. See also *ibid.,* June 21, 1894.

9. Head, 113. See also Thomasville (Georgia) *Times-Enterprise,* July 14, 1894.

10. *Age-Herald,* July 6, 1894.

11. *Ibid.,* July 7, 1894; Mobile *Daily News,* July 9, 1894; *Labor Advocate,* July 7, 1894. For a general picture see Almont Lindsay, *The Pullman Strike* (Chicago, 1942), *passim.*

12. Message to the Legislature, 1894, 40-41.

13. Jones to Erwin, July 2, 1894, Jones Papers.

14. Message to the Legislature, 1894, 41.

15. See *Report of the Adjutant General,* 60-61.

16. Message to the Legislature, 1894, 41; *Report of the Adjutant General,* 58.

17. Message to the Legislature, 1894, 41. See also Mobile *Daily News,* July 9, 1894.

18. Message to the Legislature, 1894, 41-42.

19. *Report of the Adjutant General,* 58.

20. Message to the Legislature, 1894, 42. See also *Age-Herald,* July 8,1894; Mobile *Daily News,* July 9, 1894; *Report of the Adjutant General,* 57.

21. Message to the Legislature, 1894, 42.

22. Head, 113.

23. July 11, 1894.

24. July 11, 1894.

25. Quoted in the *Age-Herald,* July 26, 1894.

26. *Labor Advocate,* July 14, 1894.

27. Bessemer *Weekly,* July 14, 1894.

28. Eugene V. Debs, *Debs: His Life, Writings and Speeches* (Chicago, 1908), 292.

29. Quoted in the Mobile *Daily News,* July 10, 1894.

30. *Age-Herald,* July 8, 1894.

31. *Ibid.,* July 13, 1894. See also Bessemer *Weekly,* July 14, 1894.

32. July 13, 1894.

33. *Age-Herald,* July 14, 1894.

34. *Labor Advocate,* July 14, 1894.

35. Telegram, Moore to Morrow, July 16, 1894, *Report of the Adjutant General,* 59. A slightly different version of the telegram is credited to L. W. Johns by the Mobile *Daily News,* July 17, 1894.

36. *Age-Herald,* July 17, 1894.

37. Mobile *Daily News,* July 17, 1894; *Age-Herald,* July 17, 1894; Message to the Legislature, 1894, 43; *Labor Advocate,* July 21, 1894.

38. *Age-Herald,* July 17, 1894; see also G. B. McCormack to Erwin, July 17, 1894, Adjutant Generals Records, Correspondence.

39. Message to the Legislature, 1894, 43.

40. *Report of the Adjutant General,* 60.

41. Mobile *Daily News,* July 17, 1894; *Report of the Adjutant General,* 61.

42. *Age-Herald,* July 19, 1894.

43. Eufaula *Times and News,* July 26, 1894.

44. *Age-Herald,* July 19, 1894; *Report of the Adjutant General,* 61.

45. July 17, 1894.

46. July 21, 1894.

47. July 21, 1894.

48. July 25, 1894.

49. July 29, 1894.

50. Message to the Legislature, 1894, 44; *Age-Herald,* July 19, 20, 1894.

51. *Ibid.,* July 20, 1894; *Labor Advocate,* July 21, 1894.

52. *Ibid.*

53. *Ibid.,* July 28, 1894.

54. Brewton *Standard Gauge,* July 19, 1894.

55. "Report of the Proceedings of the Conference between Members of the Executive Committee, United Mine Workers of Alabama and Governor Jones, called at the request of Governor Jones, July 19, 1894," Jones Papers.

56. See p. 78.

57. "Governor's Conference with the Executive Committee," Jones Papers.

58. *Ibid.*

59. *Labor Advocate,* July 14, 1894. See the report of the sheriff of Bibb County that everything was peaceful at Blocton, W. J. Latham to Jones, July 11, 1894, Adjutant General Records, Correspondence. See also *Report of the Adjutant General,* 58.

60. *Age-Herald,* July 22, 1894.

61. *Ibid.*, July 24, 1894.

62. See *Labor Advocate,* July 28, 1894.

63. Sheriff Morrow to Jones, July 25, 1894, Jones Papers.

64. E. W. to Jones, Aug 1, 1894, *ibid.* See also J. M. P. to Jones, July 20, 1894, *ibid.*

65. E. W. to Jones, Aug. 1, 1894, *ibid.*

66. See the comprehensive analysis of production and employment in the Bessemer *Weekly,* Aug. 4, 1894. See also *Labor Advocate,* July 21, 1894.

CHAPTER 7

1. See Chapter 2.

2. "Jackson" in the Montgomery *Alliance Herald,* July 7, 1893.

3. For speculation on Oates's candidacy see Prattville *Progress,* Sept. 29, 1893, quoting Birmingham *News;* Eufaula *Times and News,* Aug. 17, 1893, quoting Montgomery *Alliance Herald.*

4. Eufaula *Times and News,* Jan. 25, 1894; Troy *Jeffersonian,* Feb. 16, 1894.

5. Montgomery *Advertiser,* Feb. 8, 9, 1894; Grove Hill *Clark County Democrat,* Feb. 15, 1894; Butler *Choctaw Alliance,* May 23, 1894.

6. Union Springs *Herald,* Feb. 14, 1894. See also Camden *Wilcox Progress,* Feb. 14, 1894.

7. See Union Springs *Herald,* Feb. 14, 1894; Hayneville *Citizen Examiner,* Feb. 22, 1894.

8. Greenville *Advocate,* Mar. 29, 1894; Butler *Choctaw Alliance,* Apr. 18, 1894; Ozark *Banner,* May 16, 1894.

9. *Labor Advocate,* Mar. 17, 1894.

10. See Chapter 2.

11. Butler *Choctaw Alliance,* Mar. 14, 1894.

12. For Johnston's political views see J. F. Johnston to Robert McKee, Jan. 17, 1894, McKee Papers, Alabama Department of Archives and History, Montgomery.

13. Henry C. Oates to Thomas G. Jones, Jan. 27, 1894, Jones Papers.

14. John B. Clark, *Populism in Alabama* (Auburn, 1927), 154.

15. See Johnston's political statement, Union Springs *Herald,* May 23, 1894.

16. Butler *Choctaw Alliance,* June 20, 1894; Ozark *Banner,* May 10, 1894; Troy *Jeffersonian,* June 1, 1894.

17. See Chapter 2.

18. Jacksonville *Republican,* June 30, 1894, quoting Selma *Times.*

19. Brewton *Standard Gauge,* July 26, 1894. See also Eufaula *Times and News,* June 21, 1894.

20. *Ibid.*

21. June 23, 1894.

22. Quoted in Montgomery *Advertiser,* June 23, 1894.

23. Birmingham *Daily News,* July 26, 1894.

24. July 4, 1894.

25. *Ibid.*

26. Birmingham *Daily News,* quoted in the Union Springs *Herald,* July 18, 1894.

27. Columbiana *Shelby Sentinel,* July 12, 1894.

28. O'Neal to Senator John T. Morgan, July 8, 1894, McKee Papers.

29. *Ibid.*

30. "Sam Slim" writing in the Jacksonville *Republican,* July 21, 1894.

31. See Chapter 5.

32. *Labor Advocate,* July 7, 1894, quoting the Tuscaloosa *Journal.*

33. Troy *Jeffersonian,* Mar. 2, 1894.

34. Montgomery *Advertiser,* June 9, Nov. 16, 1894. See also Jack Abramowitz, "The Negro in the Populist Movement," *Journal of Negro History,* XXX (July, 1953), 281.

35. Hayneville *Citizen-Examiner,* July 19, 1894.

36. Jacksonville *Republican,* July 21, 1894.

37. New York *Times,* Aug. 6, 1894.

38. *Labor Advocate,* July 28, 1894.

39. See Grove Hill *Clark County Democrat,* Oct. 4, 1894; Columbiana *Shelby Sentinel,* Sept. 13, 1894.

40. See *Labor Advocate,* July 7, 1894; Bessemer *Weekly,* July 21, 1894.

41. J. N. P. to Jones, July 27, 1894, Jones Papers.

42. E. W. to Jones, July 31, 1894, *ibid.*

43. *Labor Advocate,* Aug. 4, 1894.

44. *Ibid.*

45. *Ibid.* The *Labor Advocate* is quoting a Democratic version of the affair.

46. *Ibid.*

47. Jones to Erwin, July 28, 1894, Adjutant Generals Records, Correspondence.

48. Original Manuscript Returns, Alabama Governor's Election of 1894, Alabama Department of Archives and History, Montgomery.

50. See *House of Representatives Report,* No. 572, 54 Cong., 1 Sess., *passim.*

51. Original Manuscript Returns, Alabama Governor's Election, 1892, 1894.

52. J.M.P. to Jones, Aug. 9, 1894, Jones Papers. See also Eufaula *Times and News,* Aug. 16, 1894; Montgomery *Advertiser,* Aug. 10, 24, 1894; Butler *Choctaw Alliance,* Aug. 15, 1894; Union Springs *Herald,* Aug. 29, 1894.

53. Troy *Jeffersonian,* Aug. 24, 1894.

CHAPTER 8

1. *Labor Advocate,* Aug. 4, 1894. Dennis did not think it proper to publish the lists.

2. *Ibid.*

3. Jones to Erwin, Aug. 6, 1894, Adjutant Generals Records, Correspondence.

4. *Age-Herald,* Aug. 9, 1894; E. W. to Jones, Aug. 9, 1894. Jones Papers.

5. See p. 109.

6. *Age-Herald,* Aug. 9, 1894. On the question of negotiating a general settlement or settlements with each company, see p. 110.

7. *Ibid.* See also Head, 103.

8. E. W. to Jones, Aug. 11, 1894, Jones Papers.

9. Jones to Erwin, Aug. 11, 1894, Adjutant Generals Records, Correspondence.

10. The evidence on this phase of the settlement is fragmentary. The committee referred the offer to the Tennessee Company miners prior to August 14.

11. See pp. 114-15.

12. Identification of Thomas is incomplete. A large family of that name was active in the Alabama coal and iron industry. See Armes, 175 *et passim.*

13. *Age-Herald,* Aug. 15, 1894.

14. *Ibid.*, Aug. 15, 1894.

15. Head, 104.

16. *Age-Herald,* Aug. 16, 1894; *Labor Advocate,* Aug. 18, 1894.

17. See pp. 108-09.

18. *Labor Advocate,* Aug. 18, 1894.

19. *Ibid.*

20. *Ibid.*

21. *Ibid.*

22. *Ibid.*

23. Aug. 15, 1894.

24. Aug. 23, 1894.

25. Aug. 18, 1894.

26. *Labor Advocate,* Sept. 15, 1894. Editor Dennis had earlier refused to publish the resolutions on the grounds that "the *Labor Advocate* sees no good to be derived in a public washing of royal robes
just at present. . . ." See *ibid.,* Aug. 25, 1894.

27. *Ibid.,* Sept. 15, 1894.

28. *Age-Herald,* Aug. 2, 17, 1894; Mobile *Daily News,* Sept. 24,
1894; Martha C. Mitchell, "Birmingham," 131.

29. Armes, 427.

30. Russell Houston to Jones, Oct. 1, 1894, Jones Papers.

31. Message to the Legislature, 1894, 44.

32. See Head, 105-06. For later organization efforts and discussion
of the Alabama strikes of 1904 and 1920 see Harold M. Watkins, *Coal
and Men: An Economic and Social Study of the British and American
Coalfields* (London, 1934), 215-19.

33. This includes the military expenses incurred by the state, plus
the fees and expenses paid to the Pinkerton Detective Agency. Since
a share in the maintenance and transportation of the troops was assumed by the coal companies, the final costs would total more than
$50,000. See W. A. Pinkerton to Jones, Sept. 5, 1894, Jones Papers;
Message to the Legislature, 1894, 44; *Report of the Treasurer, 1894,*
32, 45, 46, 95-98.

34. Message to the Legislature, 1894, 45.

35. *Ibid.,* 50

36. Norman Pollack, *The Populist Response to Industrial America: Midwestern Populist Thought* (Cambridge, Mass., 1962), 43.

Bibliography

PRIMARY SOURCES

Manuscripts

Adjutant Generals Records, Correspondence. Alabama Department of Archives and History, Montgomery.

Department of Agriculture Letter Books. Alabama Department of Archives and History, Montgomery.

Original Manuscript Returns, Alabama Governor's Election, 1892, 1894. Alabama Department of Archives and History, Montgomery.

Robert McKee Papers. Alabama Department of Archives and History, Montgomery.

T. A. Street Papers. University of Alabama Library, University.

Thomas Goode Jones Papers. Alabama Department of Archives and History, Montgomery.

Government Publications

Annual Report of the Treasurer of the State of Alabama, For the Fiscal Year Ending September 30, 1894. Montgomery: Brown Printing Company, 1894.

Biennial Report of the Adjutant General of Alabama to Thomas G. Jones, 1894. Montgomery: Brown Printing Company. 1894.

First Biennial Report of the Board of Inspectors of Convicts to the Governor, From September 1, 1894 to August 31, 1896. Montgomery: Roemer Printing Company, 1896.

Gibson, A. M. *Geological Survey of Alabama; Report Upon the Coosa Coal Field.* Montgomery: Roemer Printing Company, 1895.

Message of Governor Jones to the Legislature, November 14, 1894, *Journal of the House of Representatives of the State of Alabama, Session of 1894-1895.* Montgomery: Roemer Printing Company, 1895.

Message of Hon. Thos. G. Jones, Governor of Alabama, 1892. Montgomery: n.p., 1892.

Mineral Resources of the United States, 1893. Washington: Government Printing Office, 1894.

The Report of the Board of Health of the State of Alabama, For the Year 1895. Montgomery: Roemer Printing Company, 1896.

Report of the Secretary of the Interior . . . , Strikes 1882-1886. Washington: Government Printing Office, 1887.

Report of Special Committee [Alabama House of Representatives] *to Investigate Mining Industries in the State, 1897.* Montgomery: n.p., 1897.

Squire, Joseph. *Geological Survey of Alabama; Report on the Cahaba Coal Field.* Montgomery: Brown Printing Company, 1890.

Special Collections and Collected Works

Debs, Eugene. *Debs: His Life, Writings and Speeches.* Chicago: Charles H. Kerr, 1908.

Historical Collections of Birmingham, Jefferson County and Alabama: Collected, Arranged and Edited by Hill Ferguson. Birmingham Public Library, Birmingham, Alabama.

James Bowron Scrapbooks. 2 vols. Birmingham Public Library, Birmingham, Alabama.

Newspapers

Bessemer *Journal*, 1892-1894.
Bessemer *Weekly*, 1894.

Birmingham *Alabama News Digest,* 1940.
Birmingham *Age-Herald,* 1893-1894.
Birmingham *Daily News,* 1892, 1894.
Birmingham *Evening Chronicle,* 1885-1886.
Birmingham *Labor Advocate,* 1890-1894.
Birmingham *Observer,* 1880.
Birmingham *Sunday Chronicle,* 1885-1886.
Birmingham *Weekly Independent,* 1880.
Birmingham *Weekly Iron Age,* 1887.
Brewton *Standard Gauge,* 1894.
Butler *Choctaw Alliance,* 1892, 1894.
Camden *Wilcox Progress,* 1894.
Columbiana *Shelby Sentinel,* 1894.
Eufaula *Times and News,* 1892-1894.
Grove Hill *Clarke County Democrat,* 1892, 1894.
Hartselle *Alabama Enquirer,* 1887.
Hayneville *Citizen-Examiner,* 1894.
Jacksonville *Republican,* 1894.
Mobile *Daily News,* 1894.
Montgomery *Advertiser,* 1869, 1871, 1887-1888, 1890, 1892, 1894.
Montgomery *Alliance Herald,* 1893.
Moulton *Advertiser,* 1887.
New York *Times,* 1894.
Ozark *Banner,* 1894.
Prattville *Progress,* 1893.
Seale *Russell Register,* 1892.
Talladega *Our Mountain Home,* 1894.
Troy *Jeffersonian,* 1894.
Tuscaloosa *Gazette,* 1879, 1894.
Union Springs *Herald,* 1892, 1894.

SECONDARY WORKS

Articles and Theses

Abramowitz, Jack. "The Negro in the Populist Movement," *The Journal of Negro History,* XXX (July, 1953), 257-89.
Bacon, Virginia Pounds, and Nabers, Jane Porter. "The Origin of

Certain Place Names in Jefferson County, Alabama," *The Alabama Review,* V (July, 1952), 177-202.

Head, Holman. "The Development of the Labor Movement in Alabama Prior to 1900." Unpublished Master's thesis, University of Alabama, 1955.

Herr, Kincaid A. "The Louisville & Nashville Railroad, 1850-1940, 1941-1959," *L & N Magazine* (Chapters IX-XIV), 1959.

Knapp, Virginia. "William Phineas Brown, Business Man and Pioneer Mine Operator of Alabama," *The Alabama Review,* III (April, 1950; July, 1950), 108-22, 193-99.

Mitchell, Martha C. "Birmingham: Biography of a City of the New South." Unpublished Doctoral dissertation, University of Chicago, 1946.

Rogers, William W. "Agrarianism in Alabama, 1865-1896" Unpublished Doctoral dissertation, University of North Carolina, 1959.

————. "The Alabama State Grange," *The Alabama Review,* VIII (April, 1955), 104-18.

————. "The Farmers' Alliance in Alabama," *The Alabama Review,* XV (January, 1962), 5-18.

Sapp, Fannie Ella. "The Convict Lease System in Alabama, 1846-1895." Unpublished Master's thesis, George Peabody College, 1931.

Vandiver, Frank E. "Josiah Gorgas and the Brierfield Iron Works," *The Alabama Review,* III (January, 1950), 6-21.

————. "The Shelby Iron Company in the Civil War: A Case Study of a Confederate Industry," *The Alabama Review,* I (January, 1948; April, 1948; July, 1948), 12-26, 111-27, 216-17.

Woodward, Joseph H. "Alabama Iron Manufacturing, 1860-1865," *The Alabama Review,* VII (July, 1954), 199-207.

Monographs and General Works

Armes, Ethel. *The Story of Coal and Iron in Alabama.* Birmingham: The Chamber of Commerce, 1910.

Clark, John B. *Populism in Alabama.* Auburn, Alabama: Auburn Printing Company, 1927.

Couch, W. T., ed. *Culture in the South.* Chapel Hill: University of North Carolina Press, 1934.

Cruickshank, George M. *A History of Birmingham and Its Environs.* 2 vols. New York: The Lewis Company, 1920.

Evans, Chris. *History of the United Mine Workers of America.* 2 vols. N.P.: n.p., 1920.

Going, Allen J. *Bourbon Democracy in Alabama, 1874-1890.* University: University of Alabama Press, 1951.

Harnady, John R. *The Book of Birmingham.* New York: n.p., 1921.

Jefferson County and Birmingham; Historical and Biographical, 1887. Birmingham: Teagle and Smith, 1887.

Kerr, John Leeds. *The Louisville & Nashville; An Outline History.* New York: Young and Ottley, 1933.

Lindsay, Almont. *The Pullman Strike.* Chicago: University of Chicago Press, 1942.

Moss, Florence Hawkins Wood. *Building Birmingham and Jefferson County.* Birmingham: Birmingham Printing Company, 1947.

Northrup, Herbert R. *Organized Labor and the Negro.* New York: Harper and Brothers, 1944.

Pollack, Norman. *The Populist Response to Industrial America.* Cambridge: Harvard University Press, 1962.

Spero, Sterling D., and Harris, Abram L. *The Black Worker; The Negro and the Labor Movement.* New York: Columbia University Press, 1931.

Stover, John F. *The Railroads of the South, 1865-1890.* Chapel Hill: University of North Carolina Press, 1955.

Walker, Anne Kendrick. *Life and Achievements of Alfred Montgomery Shook.* Birmingham: Birmingham Publishing Company, 1952.

Watkins, Harold M. *Coal and Men; An Economic and Social Study of the British and American Coalfields.* London: n.p., 1934.

Wiebel, Arthur V. *Biography of a Business.* N.P.: Tennessee Coal and Iron Division, United States Steel Corporation, 1960.

Woodward, C. Vann. *Origins of the New South.* Baton Rouge: Louisiana State University Press, 1951.

Index